BAD BLOOD

BIRMINGHAM CITY
V ASTON VILLA

A biased Bluenose view of the rivalry

BAD BLOOD

BIRMINGHAM CITY V ASTON VILLA

A biased Bluenose view of the rivalry

Keith Dixon

This edition published in Great Britain in 2013 by DB Publishing, an imprint of JMD Media.

ISBN 9781780912356

Printed and bound by Copytech (UK) Limited, Peterborough.

CONTENTS

INTRODUCTION

I am writing this introduction on Wednesday 9 January 2013 and my wife has just said, "You get as much pleasure from the Villa losing as you do from the Blues winning". Her comments need to be put into context – Villa lost to Bradford the previous evening in the away leg of the League Cup semi-final 3–1 and face an uphill task to make the Wembley final against either Chelsea or Swansea. Bradford are currently lying 8th in League Two of the Football League whilst Villa are 16th in the Premier League. A gap of 59 places!!

The thought of Villa winning the League Cup and being relegated from the Premier League is one to cherish particularly as it was achieved by the Blues under the management of Alex McLeish (more of that betrayal later) in 2010–11 season, but the thought of the Villa being relegated and being dumped out of the League Cup at the semi-final stage is incredible. For the non-partisan reader (how come you bought this book?) you must bear in mind that most Blues fans forecast at the start of every season for Villa to be relegated regardless of what the Blues might achieve in the same season.

So my wife is right, (nothing new there!) – here I am writing my book on the rivalry between The Blues and The Villa and the first two paragraphs of this section are about the Villa losing.

But what of The Blues at the end of 2012–2013 season:

We finished in 12th position in The Championship – seven points off the Play-Offs and seven points away from relegation:

- The January transfer window saw us sell Jack Butland to Stoke City for a reported £3.5m cash deal – in the close season more high-earning squad members were sold; Nathan Redmond (a true Bluenose) to Norwich City and Curtis Davies (ex-Villa) to Hull City. Such is the confidence of the club that they initially put the previous season's top goal scorer Marlon King on the free transfer list and then settled his contract and let him leave by mutual consent!

- The club is up for sale with no firm offers on the table as at August 2013 – there is a rumour that Sammy Yiu, who was involved with Carson Yeung's takeover, is interested but that interest faded away at the start of July 2013 and he went off to try and purchase Sheffield Wednesday! A new definition of Chinese Crackers.
- The current owner is confined to Hong Kong as a condition of his bail and his assets have been frozen – his court appearances on charges of money laundering started in May 2013 and show no signs of reaching a conclusion.
- St Andrew's is no longer the fortress it was – as highlighted by the 0–5 defeat to Barnsley on 22 September 2012. At 5.00 pm we had the "bragging rights" over the Villa who had been beaten 4–0 by Southampton in a three o'clock kick-off match – leaking five second-half goals soon put an end to that!
- We cannot "wheel and deal" in the transfer market and are therefore reliant on the contributions of teenagers from the Academy – which has proved a bonus allowing the likes of Mitch Hancox, Will Packwood, Callum Reilly, Koby Arthur and Akwasi Asante to show their ability at first-team level.

- The "apprenticeship" of Jack Butland has cost us valuable points, whilst the gritty performances of Paul Robinson have been a delight – the inability of Hayden Mullins to "put a foot in" as a midfielder has been as amazing as is Lee Clark's blind spot to the player's ability. Not until Callum Reilly's debut did we see a full-blooded attempt to win the ball. Clark's reluctance to start Nikola Zigic until late into the season must have brought "sighs of relief" from our rival's defenders, because whatever your opinion of his abilities as a footballer, his physical presence gives us a massive advantage, one we were denied for most of the season.

Is it any wonder therefore that I delight in the demise of the Villa! This book is an unashamedly biased version of the Blues v Villa rivalry, which delights in all things BLUE – who knows it might stimulate a Villa version.

Although I am 66 and should know better, I find it difficult to cheer when the team is announced prior to the kick-off for those players who are ex-Villa – recently neither Curtis Davies, Liam Ridgewell or Craig Gardner have benefitted from a "hooray" from me. Having said that, I cannot bring myself to join in with the Tilton's chant to, "Sh*t on the Villa".

PREFACE

The rivalry between Blues and Villa was recognised in a *Daily Mail* survey in 2009 as the 17th greatest rivalry in club football in the world!

As is the way with the *Daily Mail* style of journalism, it chose to minimise the fundamental element of "bad blood" in local derby matches in its search to achieve its objective to make the article have more of an international appeal, big club orientation and the necessary sterility of content (remember its readership demographics) thereby enabling it to sell more newspapers.

Surely the greatest rivalry between two teams must be when both clubs involved come from the same city so whilst teams from Buenos Aires, Istanbul, Glasgow, Belgrade, Milan, Rome, Liverpool and Edinburgh may qualify to be ahead of the Birmingham teams, matches between Liverpool and Manchester United, Barcelona and Real Madrid and Amsterdam and Rotterdam do not.

The *Daily Mail* pontificated that the reasons for the rivalry lay between religion, war, political and social status.

Whilst the Glasgow rivalry is based on religion and the Belgrade hatred stimulated by previous wars, the Italians as always are fuelled by politics. Social status is the reason for the Istanbul and Buenos Aires tensions – so what is it that drives the Birmingham agenda?

To my knowledge there has never been a war involving Small Heath and Aston, although as recently as 2010 27 people were injured at the end of the Carling Cup quarter-final; although both clubs began their lives from church roots the religious connection is invalid, politics? I do not think so – but social status?

Although the Villa do not carry the city's name it has a history of success which most Bluenoses would die for, therefore it has always been able to lay claim to being the "big club" in terms of success.

Villa Park is a bigger stadium than St Andrew's and was a World Cup venue in 1966.

Villa have had a manager chosen by the Football Association to manage the England International team.

Blues v Villa derbies did not take place between 1988 and 2002 due to Blues being in a lower division than its rivals.

But beyond that the social status argument falls apart. Villa draws its support from North of the city whilst Blues' stronghold is to the South but no one would suggest that Sutton Coldfield is better than Solihull in terms of its demographic profile.

As we all know, in the main we are Blue because of our family's allegiance, which again is fundamentally linked to where you were born and/or raised. I appreciate there are families which encompass fans of both clubs but these are the exceptions which prove the rule – if your Dad was a Bluenose you are a Bluenose!

FOREWORD BY MALCOLM STENT

I've often heard it said that, we are all the victim of the place of our birth! Well I heard my dad say it quite often, and to be honest my dad was well known for being a bit of a tater, but on reflection I'm starting to think that maybe he was right. You see, I was born and bred a proud "Bluenose", nothing I could do about it, an accident of birth, born at home 111 Ellesmere Road, Saltley, Birmingham 8. The exact location of Ellesmere Road being half way up "The Rock" (Alum Rock Road) on the right between the Saltley Gate and The Rock public house.

Now it just so happens that if you were to stand at Saltley Gate with your back to the city centre, the road in front of you forks into Washwood Heath Road, to the left and Alum Rock Road to the right. Washwood Heath Road being "The Front Line", "Checkpoint Charlie", "The Wild Frontier", the natural border line between them and us and I was born and lived just a couple of hundred yards to the right, with behind us Small Heath, Bordesley Green, Sheldon and Solihull. If you listened in the geography lessons at school, you will understand that to the left of Washwood Heath Road lie Nechells, Aston, Erdington and Sutton Coldfield, the breeding grounds of "The Vile".

Being a pupil at St Saviours Church of England School, just up "The Rock" from "The Gate," meant mixing with poor, uneducated, misguided souls; in short, "the dammed" and as the mix was approximately fifty-fifty you might guess that football games at playtime (three hundred-a-side with a tennis ball, a kick every three days if you were lucky) were usually decided by a "punch-up".

The day eventually dawned when we were taken to playing fields once a week to play, and learn to play, the beautiful game. Parents were requested to supply suitable clothing (football strip) and boots. The boots, stiff-hard leather with cork toecaps; each boot took the hide of half a cow and came half way up your calf. The strip was left to the choice of each boy or his parents pocket so as you can imagine half the school wore the hallowed royal-blue and white of St Andrew's, the others minced about in the detested claret and blue or as it was known to us "washed out duck-egg and maroon". We didn't know what claret was.

If you've been concentrating, you will remember that I did say my dad, Bert, could from time to time e a bit of a tater. For some time he'd pondered on the subject of my strip. Worried that I would incur the wrath of the deadheads on the opposing side of the school, he decided that I should appear neutral and wear someone else's shirt. But who's? That was when he decided that even the colours shouldn't reflect either "The Blues" and certainly not the other lot (I still find difficulty in speaking their clubs name). Bert had long admired the skills of Len Shackleton who played for England and Sunderland. He wasn't quite sure where Sunderland was but he knew it was a long way away, far enough for no one at our school to have an axe to grind with Sunderland. His lad was safe or so he thought. Safe until the first day at the playing fields I stepped carefully out down the changing room steps resplendent in red and white striped shirt, black shorts and red and white hooped socks, every one including the teacher, Mr Brighton, fell about laughing. In the game that followed I was tripped, barged, butted, dead legged and brought down, by either side, every time the ball came my way. Unfortunately it wasn't just on the field of play, on Monday mornings after Sunderland had played Villa, if Sunderland won and Villa lost I was beaten up, If Villa won and Sunderland lost I was still beaten up even though they knew I was a Bluenose.

Over the years I've suffered the jibes, the taunts the downright abuse that I'm sure we've all had from time to time; sometimes from workmates, even from distant family members. You know the sort of thing, you just happen to mention the fact that they went down to the old third division before we did and they can't take it, they become incandescent with rage, mention May 1963 beating them in the final of the League Cup at Villa Park and it's "Mickey Mouse Cup". Along with other lads I ran on the pitch that night and used my penknife to cut a little square of their pitch to take home as a memento. We planted it in our back garden and every night before we went to bed, me and dad went out and watered it. It's a well-documented fact that the average Bluenose is a much nicer, stable, sane human being who enjoys football for the sake of the sport, we know how to lose gracefully unlike the other lot who demand success and if they don't get it, throw their toys out of the pram. They really are a thoroughly bad lot.

But for the grace of God I might have been one of them. If I'd been born just a couple of hundred yards to the left side of the Washwood Heath Road I could have been a whinger all my life and gone round shouting "Ellis Out"!! I've written a play entitled *"A League Apart"* set in May 1963 based around the famous victory mentioned earlier. The story features two families one from Small Heath the other from Sutton Coldfield who are keeping the son from Small Heath, a Bluenose, and the daughter from Sutton, one of the other lot, apart. Why are they being kept apart? Do they eventually get together? You'll have to come to see the show to find out, it's a comedy by the way full of partisan rivalry. *"A League Apart"* will be touring local theatres in the first part of April 2014. Call Brian Yeates Associates on 0121 323 2200 for details of your nearest theatre.

Finally, you know where all this rivalry started don't you ? Well I'll tell you, back in the 1870s there were two gangs of street fighters who terrorised the people of Birmingham. They were, "The Peaky Blinders, so called because they had razor blades sewn into the peaks of their flat caps enabling them to blind their opponents by taking off the cap and slashing the peak across the eyes of the foe. The Peaky's were based in Bordesley and Small Heath. The other mob were the Whitehouse Street Gang who were based, you've guessed it, in Aston. So there you have it, all this bad blood that exists between the two areas of Brum has its roots buried deep in a time before either club existed. However it's said that somewhere near the turn of the century, each gang attached itself and it's Tribalism to it's nearest football club, and we all know who they were, don't we?

BIOGRAPHY

Malcolm Stent (born 14 June 1945) is an actor, musical performer and playwright who still lives in the West Midlands. He was in a band called the Timoneers which enjoyed huge popularity during the sixties as they went from village halls to radio and TV with their unique blend of music and humour. He became the resident host of The Boggery Folk Club in Solihull taking over from Jasper Carrott.

His plays *"Go and Play up Your Own End"* – *"Play Further"* and *"A League Apart"* have been staged around the Midlands. He writes, directs and stars in the annual pantomime at the Solihull Arts Complex. He is also co-writer with Don MacLean of *"Back To Back"* and *"Wait till Your Father Gets Home"*.

ACKNOWLEDGEMENTS

My thanks to my wife, Julie, daughter Holly and son Harry, please accept my grateful thanks and apologies for any disruption to our family life. To my two older sons, Matt and Ben, thanks to them for being there together with their partners, Dell and Caz and my two grandchildren, Caleb and Amy.

My thanks also go to:

Malcolm Stent for agreeing to write the Foreword.

Mike O'Brien, my loyal archivist, for all his time in his library (attic) sorting out the support material that helps illustrate the book and also for his contribution to the "Thoughts of the Bluenoses" chapter.

Mick Sherry, my dedicated proofreader (it is St Andrew's and not St Andrews – apparently it is to do with branding!) and also for his contribution to the "Thoughts of the Bluenoses" chapter.

To my Bluenose friends whether they are former players or fans for their contributions to the book.

My father Eric, who said to me, "It ain't easy being a Bluenose but it's a lot better than following the other lot and a lot more interesting!!" and such has been the case.

The Club – I have been fortunate, if that's the expression to have supported Birmingham City football club since I was eight years of age. In those fifty-eight years I have stood on the terraces, sat in the stands and helped my club in as many ways as I possibly could:

A Scout for the Academy.

A Paying Visitor to the Corporate areas, although in all that time I have never been offered a prawn sandwich – sorry Roy Keane! (By the way why do we have an Irishman commenting on England International matches?)

A Shirt Sponsor – I still get the blame for the TRITON SHOWERS shirt of the early 1990s which was the sole responsibility of Samesh Kumar – it was meant to depict rain fall with the raindrops featuring the colours of the flag of India.

A Committee Member of the Former Player's Association under the chairmanship of Tom Ross.

A "player" for the ALL-STARS albeit it for only twenty minutes for my 60th birthday at The Lamb, Tamworth Football Club's ground against the Sheepy Old Boys.

A contributor to the now defunct *"BLUES"* magazine, where my mission was to track down ex-Blues players for a regular monthly article called "MY TIME AT THE BLUES".

An author on the club, beginning with the self-published *"THE BLUES – GREAT MATCHES – GREAT TEAMS – GREAT PLAYERS"* of which there were only 100 copies, followed by the biography of *"GIL MERRICK"* in 2009, *"BIRMINGHAM CITY – 50 GREATEST MATCHES"* in 2010 and in Summer 2011 *"BIRMINGHAM CITY – MODERN DAY HEROES"*.

Organiser of the "THE BLUENOSE EXECUTIVE LUNCH CLUB" from 10 February 2004 to 10 January 2006 inviting our heroes to lunch and chew the fat, including, in order; Ian Clarkson, Gil Merrick, Bob Hatton, Kevin Francis, Malcolm Page, Garry Pendrey, Phil Hawker, Paul Tait, Alan Campbell, Gary Sprake, John Gayle, Joe Gallagher, Robert Hopkins, Kenny Burns, Ron Wylie, Noel Blake, John Schofield, John Vincent, Tony Evans, Brian Roberts, Mick Halsall, Kevan Broadhurst, Ian Atkins, Martin Thomas and Dave Latchford.

And for the first time ever I have been able to buy a season ticket for 2013/14 as my son, Harry is no longer playing football on a Saturday afternoon since starting his university life in Sheffield. It cost me just over £200 which is about £8 per home game and I am still not getting value for money! Nothing Changes.

1

WHAT IS IT ALL ABOUT?

In his article "No Mean Rivals" in the April 1957 issue of *"Charles Buchan's Football Monthly"*, Peter Morris wrote that, "Birmingham is a city that, so far as the footballer is concerned is divided strictly in two. The east takes in the stately red brick of Villa Park – hard by historic Aston Hall where on dusky winter afternoons you may catch a ghostly glimpse of a bewhiskered Villa giant of a bygone era. Directly across the city from Villa Park, over the grey smoking factory area fringing the Aston New Road, and on to Small Heath, they have built a new St Andrew's out of the war debris and with it a new Birmingham City club. It is here, around Bordesley Green, up to Muntz Street and down the Coventry Road as far as Sheldon that you will find the royal blue and white of Birmingham City. Their supporters are sworn enemies of the claret and light blue of Witton and Perry Barr, Erdington and the immediate regions of Handsworth, where you may, unless you are careful, bump into the alien stripes of West Bromwich Albion. For a long, long while aristocratic Aston Villa were the permanent top dogs in "Brum". Everyone knew that and Villa men gazed across their city with lofty amusement at the small fry in Small Heath. Times change – the wheel has turned full circle. Birmingham City these days are a power in the land. And so to the future…the endless arguments…the brave words in pubs and club…the loyalties that have never flagged and never will".

That article was written a month before the Villa won the FA Cup against the post-Munich Manchester United team and the wheel turned once again in the favour of Aston.

Over the years Blues v Villa became the derby that football forgot and the fans yearned for, as success (or lack of it!) on the pitch, meant that the two clubs were in different leagues. No other big city rivalry had to wait as long for its protagonists to renew the duel for league supremacy as the Birmingham one. December 12, 1987 was the date of the match in the Second Division in front of 28,000 at St Andrew's, which heralded a wait of fifteen years before

Blues could resume its league rivalry with the Villa. The main reason for the wait was that that season saw Villa promoted and for Blues, things got much worse before the Gold and Sullivan era began the transformation which put the club where it belonged in the top division, although the stay in the Premier was all too short.

Unlike other inter-city rivalries – beyond the confines of Birmingham it isn't remembered for the football and even those in the respective camps would acknowledge a dearth of sporting memories. Blues v Villa is best known as a public order problem. Meetings in the early 1980s would see an average of around 50 arrests for violence and a couple of pubs routinely destroyed.

The tendency of Birmingham's teams to underachieve is behind the derby's lack of a genuine sporting tradition. Birmingham City are famous for never having won anything of value until the Carling Cup victory in 2011, whilst the Villa fans (what do they call themselves? I have never heard them call themselves anything) live off past glories, even claiming that they have had the FA Cup stolen more times than we have won it!

One of the tastiest derbies took place at St Andrew's in December 1982, when Villa were reigning European Champions. At the start of that year, the legendary title-winning Villa manager Ron Saunders suddenly resigned, only to resurface at Birmingham City to replace the sacked Jim Smith. The Christmas fixture was his first derby as a Bluenose, and he had already raided Villa reserves for Noel Blake.

David Gough, a Blues fan for over 30 years, recalls: "Nearly 44,000 supporters were crammed into St Andrew's that day and it was an impressive sight, one I have never forgotten. The noise was unbelievable – I was at the back of the Spion Kop and you could not hear the Villa fans singing. You could see their arms move and point towards the Blues fans, so they were singing, but the noise in the Kop just drowned it out." It got even noisier during the first half when Blake put Blues one up with a rare goal, and a rattled Villa conceded two more during the second period to put the seal on a thoroughly humiliating afternoon."

Whilst the Blues v Villa rivalry has not thrown up anywhere near as many stories or incidents as, say, the Liverpool or Manchester confrontations. Those that have occurred are provoked by a genuine feeling of bad blood between the two sets of supporters, such as the time when Blues' Paul Tait (who was sent off against the Villa in a League Cup tie in 1993) removed his jersey after the 1995 Auto Windscreens Shield Final at Wembley to brandish a "Shit on the Villa" T-shirt in front of gleeful cameramen. The stunt went down well with Blues fans, but for the Villa fans (do they really call themselves "Villans") it merely confirmed a lot of prejudices held about Bluenoses.

For many Villa fans those prejudices are extreme which to some extent is understandable when you consider that a regular chant at every Blues home game is: *"Shit on the Villa, Shit on the Villa tonight, Shit on the Villa, Shit on the Villa tonight, Shit on the Villa, Shit on the Villa tonight, Everyone shit on the Villa, because they are a load of sh-ite"*

I find it difficult to sing that chant, although I will bellow *"Keep Right On"*, *"We don't care about Carson"* and *"Stand Up"* etc., because I want to support the Blues team on the pitch rather than sing a rant against Villa who I do not want to think about when I am at St Andrew's.

These prejudices are also reflected in the way the fans describe themselves: Bluenoses are fervently passionate about their working-class status and are happy to consider Villa fans to be more "toff-like". A bit like the Manchester Clubs where United's fan base tends to be outside of the city's boundaries and City's support-ers are the real "Mancs" the same could be said of Blues and Villa – Blues fans are more likely to live in the city itself, while Villa attract a more widely spread crowd. The reality is that nothing is as clearly defined as that, with truth being that each club's support is drawn from a very similar social background.

The Birmingham derby is full of bad blood. It's totally driven by hate and much of that comes down to Blues years of looking up at Villa and the sub-sequent desire to show them who is the best. It's an intense bad blood-boiling rivalry between people who work together drink together and even live to-gether. Nobody on the outside will ever quite understand it. Why? Because it is illogical, eg;

- Taking six points from two derby games in a season is the main target for any season – everything else is treated as a bonus.
- I do not care how the Blues do as long as the Villa get relegated.

BLUES QUIZ

This chapter is designed to "programme" the reader, particularly those who are not Bluenoses to the fact that the content of the book is totally biased to Birmingham City Football Club and totally against Aston Villa Football Club. To demonstrate this mentality remember Blues have played the Villa 116 times and Blues have recorded 38 wins and 29 draws – in Bad Blood there will no references to the defeats (naturally) or the draws (as Villa got a point off us). Therefore in Chapter Three I only recognise Blues' victories over the Villa.

In order to ensure the correct mentality is achieved before progressing to Chapter Three, the reader must complete the BLUES QUIZ, which is so called because the answer to each question is "THE BLUES"

QUIZ QUESTION NUMBER ONE

Who has had the most sponsors since 1983? The Blues or The Villa? Answer: THE BLUES.

BLUES WIN 15–13

YEAR	BLUES
1984–85	ANSELLS
1985–86	ULTRABRITE
1986–87	CO-OP MILK
1987–88	P.J. EVANS
1988–89	EVANS HALSHAW
1989–92	MARK ONE
1992–95	TRITON SHOWERS
1995–2001	AUTO WINDSCREENS
2001–03	PHONES 4 U
2003–04	FLYBE
2004–07	FLYBE.COM

2007–11	F & C INVESTMENTS
2011–12	RATIONALFX
2012–13	EZE GROUP
2013–	NICOLITES

In the same period for the Villa: Davenports, Mita, Muller, AST Computer, LDV, NTL, DWS Investments, 32red.com, Acorns Childrens' Hospice, FxPro, Genting Casinos, Databet.

QUIZ QUESTION NUMBER TWO

Who has had the most changes of kit since 1975? The Blues or The Villa? Answer: THE BLUES.

BLUES WIN 13–11

YEAR	BLUES
1975–77	UMBRO
1977–82	ADIDAS
1982–86	PATRICK
1986–91	MATCHWINNER
1991–93	INFLUENCE
1993–96	ADMIRAL
1996–98	PONY
1998–04	LE COQ SPORTIF
2004–05	DIADORA
2005–07	LONSDALE
2007–10	UMBRO
2010–12	XTEP
2012–	DIADORA

In the same period for the Villa: Umbro, Le Coq Sportif, Henson, Hummel, Umbro, Asics, Reebok, Diadora, Hummel, Nike, Macron.

QUIZ QUESTION NUMBER THREE

Who has had the most owners in its history? The Blues or The Villa? Answer: THE BLUES.

BLUES WIN 7–3

	BLUES	
1	July 1988	Local businessmen and dignitaries
2	1965	Clifford Coombs
3	1975	Keith Coombs
4	1985	Ken Wheldon
5	1991	Kumar Brothers
6	1993	Sullivan & Golds
7	2007	Carson Yeung

	VILLA	
1	End of 19th Century	Local businessmen and dignitaries
2	1968	Doug Ellis
3	2006	Randy Lerner

QUIZ QUESTION NUMBER FOUR

Who had the most grounds in their history? The Blues or The Villa? Answer: THE BLUES.

BLUES WIN 4–3

Arthur Street, Bordesley Green

Ladypool Road, Sparkbrook

Muntz, Street

St Andrew's

(Villa – Aston Park, Wellington Road, Perry Barr and Villa Park).

QUIZ QUESTION NUMBER FIVE

Who had the most names in their history? The Blues or The Villa? Answer: THE BLUES.

BLUES WIN 4–1
Small Heath Alliance in 1875
Small Heath Football Club Limited in 1888
Birmingham in 1905
Birmingham City in 1943.

QUIZ QUESTION NUMBER SIX

Which club with a Birmingham postcode was the only English Club to win a competitive game at Milan's San Siro stadium until Arsenal equalled the feat 40 years after in 2001? The Blues or The Villa? Answer: THE BLUES.

QUIZ QUESTION NUMBER SEVEN

Which club with a Birmingham postcode proved to be politically correct and appoint a female to their Board of Directors? The Blues or The Villa? Answer: THE BLUES (For those Bluenoses who have lived on a desert island since 1993 – Karren Brady).

Karren Brady modelling a TRITON shirt in Sunday Times magazine

QUIZ QUESTION NUMBER EIGHT

Which club with a Birmingham postcode provided fundamental evidence to Mr Justice Popplewell's inquiry into safety at sports ground in 1985? The Blues or The Villa?

Answer: BLUES – The last home game of the 1984–85 promotion season against Leeds United was marred by rioting which culminated in the death of a boy when a wall collapsed on him. This was the same day as the Bradford City stadium fire and the two incidents formed part of the remit to Popplewell.

QUIZ QUESTION NUMBER NINE

In the Premiership season of 2003–04 who was the team with a Birmingham postcode that made the fewest fouls? The Blues or The Villa? Answer: THE BLUES.

In 2003/04 Villa committed 609 fouls – the highest in the Premiership. In this book that made them the dirtiest team in the country.

QUIZ QUESTION NUMBER TEN

Which club with a Birmingham postcode has qualified for The Europa League Competition? The Blues or The Villa? Answer: THE BLUES.

Right you are now programmed and will be able to enjoy the rest of the book!

THE VICTORIES

These are victories achieved in senior league and cup competitions – victories gained in friendly matches etc. are included elsewhere:

1.	16 September 1905	20.	27 May 1963
2.	20 January 1906	21.	30 March 1964
3.	19 January 1907	22.	7 October 1967
4.	18 January 1908	23.	24 February 1968
5.	15 March 1922	24.	21 September 1968
6.	17 March 1923	25.	3 April 1976
7.	25 August 1923	26.	18 September 1976
8.	11 October 1924	27.	10 May 1977
9.	27 February 1926	28.	1 October 1977
10.	9 March 1929	29.	25 February 1978
11.	8 March 1933	30.	27 December 1982
12.	25 August 1934	31.	31 March 1984
13.	29 October 1938	32.	22 March 1986
14.	4 December 1948	33.	22 August 1987
15.	24 August 1957	34.	16 September 2002
16.	21 December 1957	35.	3 March 2003
17.	20 December 1958	36.	12 December 2004
18.	28 October 1961	37.	20 March 2005
19.	27 October 1962	38.	1 December 2010

VICTORY – NUMBER ONE

- 16 September 1905 – Muntz Street – Crowd: 30,000 – First Division
- WON 2-0 – scorers – Mounteney and Jones
- This game was the first game played under the name Birmingham and was our first league win over the Villa, who had beaten us seven times previously.

1905 Team Group with Mayor of Birmingham's Charity Cup

Team:
A.C. ROBINSON, J.W. GLOVER, F. STOKES, W.J. BEER, W. WIGMORE, J. DOUGHERTY, B.H. GREEN, A. MOUNTENEY, W.H. JONES, F.J. WILCOX, C.W.F. FIELD

The Villa team that capitulated on that day was:
Billy George, Alec Leake, Freddie Mills, Howard Spencer, Albert Wilkes, Jack Windmill, Albert Hall, Billy Brown, Harry Hampton, Billy Garraty and Joe Bache.

VICTORY – NUMBER TWO

- 20 January 1906 – Villa Park – Crowd: 40,000 – First Division
- WON 3–1 – scorers – Mounteney, Dougherty and Jones

Team:

A.C. ROBINSON, J.W. GLOVER, A.W. HARTWELL, F. CORNAN,
W. WIGMORE, J. DOUGHERTY, R. HARPER, B.H. GREEN, W.H. JONES,
A. MOUNTENEY, G. ANDERSON

The Villa team that capitulated on that day was:

Billy George, Michael Noon, Alec Leake, Albert Evans, Albert Wilkes, Joe
Pearson, Albert Hall, Billy Brown, Harry Hampton, Billy Garraty and Joe
Bache.

- FIRST LEAGUE DOUBLE OVER THE VILLA

VICTORY – NUMBER THREE

- 19 January 1907 – St Andrew's – Crowd: 50,000 – First Division
- WON 3–2 – scorers – Glover, Mounteney and Green
- This game was the third game played at St Andrew's

Team:

A.C. ROBINSON, J.W. GLOVER, F. STOKES, W.J. BEER, W. WIGMORE,
F. CORNAN, R. HARPER, B.H. GREEN, W.H. JONES, A. MOUNTENEY,
G. ANDERSON

The Villa team that capitulated on that day was:

Billy George, James Logan, Walter Corbett, Sam Greenhalgh, Roland
Codling, Chris Buckley, Bob Evans, James Cattrell , Harry Hampton,
Joe Walters (1) and Fred Chapple.

- The Birmingham winner came from a hotly disputed penalty. Referee F.
  Kirkham of Preston was roundly abused and his award described in print
  as "a grievous wrong to Villa".

- In 1906–07 season Blues beat Aston Villa 4–0 in the Final of the Lord Mayor of Birmingham Charity Shield.

St.Andrew's in 1906

VICTORY – NUMBER FOUR

- 18 January 1908 – Villa Park– Crowd: 39,500 – First Division
- WON 3–2 – scorers – Green, Drake and Eyre

Team:
J. DORRINGTON, W.S. CORBETT, J.H. KEARNS, W. WIGMORE,
W.J. BEER, B.H. GREEN, C.H. TICKLE, E. BLUFF, A. MOUNTENEY,
A. DRAKE, E. EYRE

The Villa team that capitulated on that day was:
Billy George, James Logan (1), Tommy Lyons, Freddie Miles, Roland
Codling, Albert Hall (1) , Rowland Harper, Billy Garraty, Harry Hampton,
Joe Bache and Alec Logan.

- 1907–1908 season saw Blues' first £1,000 transfer with the move of Alonso Drake from Sheffield United.
- Walter Corbett won a gold medal for Football in the 1908 Olympics.
- Blues retained the Lord Mayor of Birmingham Charity Cup beating Villa 5–2.

VICTORY – NUMBER FIVE
- 15 March 1922 – St Andrew's – Crowd: 34,190 – First Division
- WON 1–0 – scorer – Crosbie

Team:
D. TREMELLING, J. ROULSON, J. JONES, G. LIDDELL, A. McCLURE,
P. BARTON, J. BARRATT, J. CROSBIE, J. BRADFORD, H. HAMPTON,
F. FOXALL

The Villa team that capitulated on that day was:
Tommy Jackson, Percy Jones, Ernest Blackburn, Frank Barson, George
Blackburn, Arthur Dorrell, Richard York, Ian Dickson, John Johnstone, Billy
Walker and Billy Kirton.

- Season 1921–22 was infamous as Blues did not participate in the FA Cup
  due to its registration forms arriving too late for entry.
- Johnny Crosbie became the first Blues' player to be capped for Scotland –
  the match was against England in April 1922 at Villa Park.
- We played the Villa twice in one week as we drew 1–1 away on 11 March
  1922 – so unbeaten over two games in the same week.

VICTORY – NUMBER SIX
- 17 March 1923 – St Andrew's – Crowd: 50,000 – First Division
- WON 1–0 – scorer – Rawson

Team:
D. TREMELLING, E.A. ASHURST, J. JONES, J. DAWES, A. McCLURE,
P. BARTON, W.H.T. HARVEY, J. CROSBIE, A.G. RAWSON, J. BRADFORD,
W. CLARK

The Villa team that capitulated on that day was:
Cyril Spiers, Thomas Ball, Tommy Smart, Tommy Mort, George Blackburn,
Frank Moss, Arthur Dorrell, Richard York, Billy Walker, Joe Roxburgh and
Len Capewell.

- Played two games in the same week with the away fixture on 24 March 1923.

VICTORY – NUMBER SEVEN
- 25 August 1923 – St Andrew's – Crowd: 41,306 – First Division
- WON 3–0 – scorers – Clarke and Bradford 2

Team:
D. TREMELLING, E.A. ASHURST, J. JONES, R.A. DALE, A. McCLURE, P. BARTON, W.H.T. HARVEY, J. CROSBIE, J. BRADFORD, M. LANE, W. CLARKE

The Villa team that capitulated on that day was:
Cyril Spiers, Thomas Ball, Tommy Smart, Tommy Mort, George Blackburn, Frank Moss, Arthur Dorrell, Richard York, Ian Dickson, Billy Walker, and Billy Kirton.

- Opening day win for the Blues!

VICTORY – NUMBER EIGHT
- 11 October 1924 – St Andrew's – Crowd: 48,098 – First Division
- WON 1–0 – scorer – Islip

Team:
D. TREMELLING, F. WOMACK, J. JONES, G. LIDDELL, J. CRINGAN, P. BARTON, W.H.T. HARVEY, J. CROSBIE, J. BRADFORD, G. ISLIP, A. SCRIVEN

The Villa team that capitulated on that day was:
Cyril Spiers, Tommy Smart, Tommy Mort, Victor Milne, George Blackburn, Frank Moss, Arthur Dorrell, Richard York, Billy Walker, Len Capewell and Billy Kirton.

- Season 1924–25 Blues finished eighth with the Villa finishing 15th.

VICTORY – NUMBER NINE

- 27 February 1926 – St Andrew's – Crowd: 38,231 – First Division
- WON 2–1 – scorers – Briggs 2

1926-27 Team Group

Team:

D. TREMELLING, F. WOMACK, J. JONES, G. LIDDELL, B. HUNTER, R.A. DALE, W.N. HARRIS, J. CROSBIE, G.R. BRIGGS, T.LINLEY, C. RUSSELL

- In the reverse fixture Blues scored three goals in the last 11 minutes at Villa Park to draw 3–3

Match Report

"With only eleven minutes to go the star-studded Villa were winning 3–0 on their own ground. Thousands were already spilling out on to Trinity Road, homeward bound. All over? No…in a sensational finish Birmingham fought back to equalise 3–3 with the referee looking at his watch. In the first half, Walker and Dorrell on the left, and York and Kirton on the right, had bewildered the Birmingham defence. The home attack were playing brilliant football. Villa had started the season – the first under the new offside rule – by thrashing Burnley 10–0 at Villa Park. They looked entirely capable of repeating the performance against "The Blues". In ten minutes Billy Walker gave them the lead. Five minutes before half-time the famous Walker corkscrew legs outwitted Frank Womack and Villa led 2–0. After 65 minutes Capewell got a third despite fervent Birmingham appeals for offside. Then came the game's turning point, Doctor Vic Milne, the six-foot amateur centre-half from Aberdeen, was injured and Birmingham's Joe Bradford began to see more of the ball. With 11 minutes left, Joe snapped up a Tommy Mort miskick and scored. Two minutes later it was Bradford again. 3–2 and the Birmingham players raced to the centre spot for the kick-off. Milne was now limping on the Villa left wing, Frank Moses went to centre-half and Walker to left-half in a bid to stem the blue and white tide. All in vain. And with six minutes to go came tragedy for the Villa crowd. Goalkeeper Cyril Spiers went to stop a long shot and slipped. In trying to push the ball away he only succeeded in throwing it into his own net. 3–3 and pandemonium on the terraces. Birmingham had scored three times in five minutes! Honour was preserved. After the match Cyril Spiers admitted it was his fault: 'But I did not slip. I thought the ball was going wide, but it hit someone and instead went just inside the post."

VICTORY – NUMBER TEN

- 9 March 1929 – Villa Park – Crowd: 56,528 – First Division
- WON 2–1 – scorers – Crosbie and Mills

Team:
H. HIBBS, E. BARKAS, J. RANDLE, G. LIDDELL, G.R. MORRALL, A.J. LESLIE, G.R. BRIGGS, J. CROSBIE, B.R. MILLS, J. BRADFORD G. HICKS

The Villa team that capitulated on that day was:
Ben Olney, Tommy Smart, Tommy Mort, Alec Talbot, Joe Tate, James Gibson, Arthur Dorrell, Richard York, Pongo Waring, Joe Beresford and Billy Walker.

VICTORY– NUMBER ELEVEN
- 8 March 1933 – St Andrew's – Crowd: 24,868 – First Division
- WON 3–2 – scorers – Briggs, Grosvenor and Bradford

Team:

H. HIBBS, H. BOOTON, E. BARKAS, L. STOKER, G.R. MORRALL,
C.F. CALLADINE, G.R. BRIGGS, A.T. GROSVENOR, J. BRADFORD,
R.E. GREGG, E.R. CURTIS

- Blues won the Lord Mayor of Birmingham Charity Cup for the fourth time beating the Villa 2–0.

Match Report

Blues received an early boost to this long awaited derby clash against Villa with the return to the side of striker Joe Bradford out since the game against Newcastle on 27 December, and it was Bradford who kicked off against an unchanged and full-strength Villa side.

Birmingham soon got into their stride and looked the better of the two sides in the opening 15 minutes. Two efforts from Gregg came close to opening the scoring but Villa's goal attempts were restricted to long-range efforts. The best of these was a 20-yard free kick which was acrobatically tipped over the bar by Hibbs. The Villa 'Keeper (Morton) then saved brilliantly to deny Briggs from a point-blank shot with his chest. The Blues pressure continued and Morton saved expertly again from Morrall. Hibbs at the other end was enjoying the game in virtual spectator mode, but he had to be alert soon after the half-hour mark when he twice made vital contributions to keep the Blues goal intact. In an end-to-end game Briggs was presented with the best chance so far by a great pass from Grosvenor, however with just Morton in front of him he sliced his shot horribly wide. Briggs soon made amends when he grabbed a dramatic goal just before half-time much to the delight of the 50,000 St Andrew's crowd. Another teasing chipped centre from Grosvenor was headed on by Bradford for Curtis to hit on the volley, Morton flung himself to the right to pull off yet another magnificent save, but Briggs reacted quickly to knock in the rebound to give Blues' a 1–0 interval lead.

There was a sensational start to the second half when Bradford conjured up a moment of magic to put Blues 2–0 up. A long ball out of defence from Stoked found Grosvenor. Taking the ball wide he crossed for Bradford in the centre, taking the ball in his stride the centre-forward placed the ball into the far corner of the net beyond the despairing dive of Morton. Bradford was back with a trademark finish and Blues scented victory. Now it was all Birmingham pressure and only desperate defending was preventing their forwards from running riot. But from a breakaway Villa got themselves back in the game against the run of play. A superb ball from Houghton set up the chance for Brown who rushed through a non-existent defence to easily put pass HIbbs. What a change this had on the game, as suddenly it was Villa who threatened to score with every forward pass. Twice HIbbs came to the rescue as Villa piled men forward seeking an equaliser. But in similar circumstances to Villa's goals, it was Birmingham who restored their two goal advantage after 62 minutes. Curtis this time set up the chance by squaring the ball to Grosvenor who hammered a first time shot which gave Morton no chance of stopping. Blues almost increased their lead soon after with close efforts from Briggs then Bradford as the Villa goal fell under siege. Villa to their credit continued to battle away and earned a consolation reward with five minutes remaining when the Blues defence faltered a second time. After a strange bout of head tennis within the penalty area Mandley nipped in to win the ball and head past Hibbs. Villa pressed right up to the final whistle, but Blues held on to claim a victory in this the 40th Second City derby. Blues now had 11 wins.

VICTORY – NUMBER TWELVE

- 25 August 1934 – St.Andrew's – Crowd: 53,930 – First Division
- WON 2–1 – scorers – Harris and Guest

Team:
H. HIBBS, H. BOOTON, A. HUBBARD, L. STOKER, G.R. MORRALL, C.F. CALLADINE, S. MOFFATT, F. HARRIS, D. MANGNALL, J. BRADFORD, W.F. GUEST

The Villa team that capitulated on that day was:

Harry Morton, George Beeson, Tommy Mort, James Allen, Tom Gardner, James Gibson, Eric Houghton, Arthur Cunliffe, Pongo Waring (1), Dai Astley and Ronnie Dix.

- Another opening day win over the Villa.

VICTORY – NUMBER THIRTEEN

- 29 October 1938 – St Andrew's – Crowd: 55,301 – First Division
- WON 3–0 – scorers – Brown and Harris 2

Team:

F.E. CLACK, C. TRIGG, W.M. HUGHES, D.J. DEARSON, W.G. HALSALL, D.T. RICHARDS, F.R.H. WHITE, D.B. JENNINGS, C. PHILLIPS, F. HARRIS, J. BROWN

Match Report

Over 55,000 jammed the St Andrew's slopes on a crisp autumn afternoon when Villa fielded their promotion side for the first time since the season's opening game. After 25 minutes Bob Iverson was injured and Birmingham took command. On 62 minutes Fred Harris put Blues ahead and with fifteen minutes to go a Jackie Brown long shot made it 2–0. With four minutes left it was Harris again with a perfect header from a free-kick.

Official BCFC autograph sheet circa 1948

VICTORY – NUMBER FOURTEEN

- 4 December 1948 – Villa Park – Crowd: 62,424 – First Division
- WON 3–0 – scorers – Bodle and Stewart 2

Team:

G. MERRICK, K. GREEN, D.B. JENNINGS, F. HARRIS, E. DUCKHOUSE,
F. MITCHELL, J. BERRY, J. STEWART, N. DOUGALL, H. BODLE,
H. ROBERTS

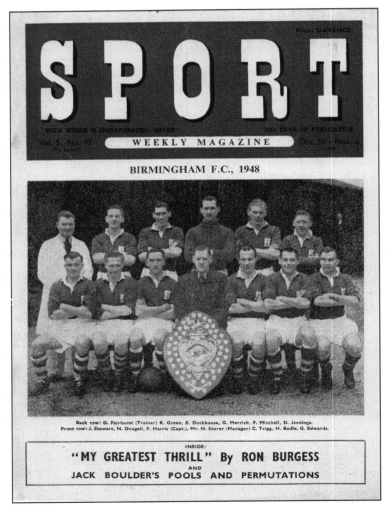

Cover of Sport Weekly Magazine featuring Birmingham F.C.

- Jackie Stewart, the chunky little Scot from Raith Rovers, was tried at inside-right and scored two beautiful goals. Firebrand Trevor Ford leading the Villa attack was allowed hardly a kick by big Ted Duckhouse.

Match Report

This was the first Second City derby in the league since March 1939 and little wonder there was a bumper crown packed into Villa Park. But, as the *Sports Argus* banner headlines proclaimed it was "St Andrew's Day at Villa Park".

It was actually four days after the official day for Scotland's patron saint, but that didn't bother Jackie Stewart, the stocky Scottish winger who netted two of Blues' goals (both from inside-forward) with Harold Bodle claiming the other.

Only four players – two from each side – had survived from the last pre-war derby: goalkeeper Joe Rutherford and full-back George Cummings for Villa and Fred Harris and Dennis Jennings from Blues, who in 1939, had formed the right wing but were now right-half and left-back respectively.

Faced by a Villa attack led by the fiery figure of Welsh international Trevor Ford, and with St Andrew's favourite Jock Mulraney on the right-wing. Blues' defence played exceedingly well throughout, restricting the men in claret and blue to only three efforts on goal in the first half (two from George Edwards) and two in the second half (both from Ford).

In contrast, Blues themselves, using the long-ball game in contrast to Villa's short-passing approach, attacked with confidence, with the 24-year-old Stewart, signed from Raith Rovers, in devastating form.

He scored the opening goal on 15 minutes rounding off a flowing move which originated with Ted Duckhouse deep in Blues' territory. Stewart, in the inside-left position, took a clever back-heeler by Neil Dougall before going on to beat Joe Rutherford with a well-place shot to the goalkeeper's right.

Stewart's second goal arrived on 66 minutes. He popped up in the right place at the right time to hook the ball wide of Rutherford from a set piece involving Harris, who took the free-kick, and Bodle, whose header left Stewart free eight yards from goal. At this stage Blues were in total control of the game and they added a third goal on 71 minutes when Bodle, who had had a fine match, tucked away a chance created by outside-right Johnny Berry, Bodle netting with a cleverly flighted lob over the advancing goalkeeper.

VICTORY – NUMBER FIFTEEN

- 24 August 1957 – St Andrew's – Crowd: 50,780 – First Division
- WON 3–1 – scorers – Brown, Kinsey and Murphy

Team:

J. SCHOFIELD, J. HALL, K. GREEN, J. WATTS, T. SMITH, R. NEAL,
G. ASTALL, N. KINSEY, E. BROWN, P. MURPHY, A. GOVAN

The Villa team that capitulated on that day was:

Nigel Sims, Stan Lynn, Peter Aldis, Jimmy Dugdale, Pat Saward, Stan
Crowther, Peter McParland (1), Les Smith, Jackie Sewell, Johnny Dixon, Billy
Myerscough.

Trevor Smith and Johnny Dixon - The Captains

- Yet another opening day for the Blues over the Villa.
- 1957–58 Season Blues finished 13th in Division One, one place above the Villa.
- This was Blues' first home victory over Villa in 19 years.
- As a bonus Villa were the reigning FA Cup holders.

VICTORY – NUMBER SIXTEEN

- 21 December 1957 – Villa Park – Crowd: 41,118 – First Division
- WON 2–0 – scorers – Brown and Kinsey

Team:
G. MERRICK, J. HALL, B. FARMER, B. LARKIN, T. SMITH, R. NEAL, H. HOOPER, N. KINSEY, E. BROWN, P. MURPHY, G. ASTALL

Programme 21st December 1957

Eddie Brown beats Jimmy Dugdale

The Villa team that capitulated on that day was:
Nigel Sims, Stan Lynn, Peter Aldis, Jimmy Dugdale, Pat Saward, Stan
Crowther, Vic Crowe, Peter McParland, Les Smith, Gerry Hitchens and
Johnny Dixon.

- Our first double over the Villa for over 50 years!
- The icing on the cake was that we finished 13th that year one place ahead
  of our rivals.

VICTORY – NUMBER SEVENTEEN
- 20th December 1958 – St Andrew's – Crowd: 31,857 – First Division
- WON 4–1 – scorers – Neal, Astall (pen) and Jackson 2

Team:
G. MERRICK, J. HALL, G. ALLEN, J. WATTS, T. SMITH, R. NEAL,
G. ASTALL, J. GORDON, A. JACKSON, B. LARKIN, B. TAYLOR

The Villa team that capitulated on that day was:
Nigel Sims, Stan Lynn, Peter Aldis, Jimmy Dugdale, Vic Crowe, Peter McParland, Les Smith, Walter Hazeldean (1), Jackie Sewell, Johnny Dixon and Billy Myerscough.

Programme 20th December 1958

- 1958–59 Season Blues finished 9th in Division One with the Villa relegated in 21st position.

VICTORY – NUMBER EIGHTEEN

- 28 October 1961 – Villa Park – Crowd: 39,790 – First Division
- WON 3–1 – scorers – Orritt and Harris 2

Team:

J. SCHOFIELD, S. LYNN, G. SISSONS, T. HENNESSEY, T. SMITH, M. BEARD, M. HELLAWELL, J. BLOOMFIELD, J. HARRIS, B. ORRITT, B. AULD

The Villa team that capitulated on that day was:

Geoff Sidebotton, John Neal, Charlie Aitken, John Sleeuwenhoek, Vic Crowe, Mike Tindall, Alan Deakin, Harry Burrows, Peter McParland (1), Norman Ashe and Ron Wylie.

- In the reverse fixture in March 1962 Auld and Dugdale went off injured following a "clash of heads".

Programme 28th October 1961

VICTORY -NUMBER NINETEEN

- 27 October 1962 – St Andrew's – Crowd: 42,207 – First Division
- WON 3–2 – scorers – Lynn (pen) and Leek 2

Team:
C. WITHERS, S. LYNN, G. SISSONS, J. WATTS, T. SMITH, T. HENNESSEY, M. HELLAWELL, R. STUBBS, J. HARRIS, K. LEEK, B. AULD

Match Report

A crowd of 42,207, the largest gate of the season, watched this nail-biting duel as Birmingham City met Aston Villa in their 17th post-war league game. Villa made the early running and Withers did well to cut out a Ewing centre.

The first Blues pressure came after Hellawell was impeded, but Leek just failed to get his head to the cross. The Blues won three right-wing corners in as many minutes, but Villa were able to cut out the threat in the penalty area. In the 11th minute a back-pass from Watts was intercepted by O'Neill. The inside-right chipped it across to Thomson, but Lynn raced back to clear from the line. After 15 minutes, Villa had the slight edge, although neither team had settled down.

Ken Leek scores against the Villa

Hennessey worked well for Blues, doing a lot if fetching and carrying. In the 18th minute a Wylie pass cleared the way for O'Neill, but he failed to control the ball properly, and the opportunity was lost. This was followed by a free kick to Blues on the edge of penalty area. Auld screwed the ball across, but Sidebottom lunged to flip it clear, and Aitken completed the clearance to thwart the on-rushing Hellawell. Burrows had shown little of his form so far, but in the 25th minute he outpaced Lynn and hooked the ball into the centre where Hennessey was able to intercept an O'Neill challenge. Then Auld showed Lee a fine pair of heels to find the head of Harris with a perfect cross, but the centre-forward failed to collect cleanly and the ball went past the right hand post. In the 32nd minute Auld again centred along the face of the goal from the by-line. But Harris, only a couple of yards out, missed a chance when the ball skidded off the side of his foot for a goal-kick. Villa were the better side as the half progressed. Ewing had a shot rebound off the far post, but Thomson spoiled the chance by moving offside. Then Ewing again flashed though to Wylie, but the inside-left overran the ball. The first half ended Birmingham City 0 Aston Villa 0.

The first chance of the second half fell to Blues when Auld forced an opening and Leek headed his centre down to Stubbs, who had plenty of time to turn and shoot, but put it wide. It was Villa who broke the deadlock in the 55th minute. Aitken robbed Harris and sent the ball to Thomson in midfield. Spotting O'Neill, Thomson passed immediately, and O'Neill moved in to fire past Withers. Only four minutes later, Auld, who had just beaten three Villa defenders, was brought down in the penalty area by Sleeuwenhoek. Lynn took the penalty kick and equalised. The Villa regained the lead when Burrows also scored from the penalty spot, the result of Smith holding off Thomson. With the tension almost at breaking point, Auld then took a free-kick on the left and floated the ball across to Leek, and the Blues man out jumped everyone to head the ball in via the near post. Four goals in six minutes. Sidebottom was injured in the process, and four minutes stoppage time was incurred as he received treatment. He eventually resumed and moments later was able to clear a header from Stubbs. Then Villa broke clear to win a corner, But Burrows' in swinger was saved by Withers on the near post. In the 73rd minute Leek put Blues ahead for the first time. Auld chipped over a left-wing corner, and while several Villa players hesitated, Leek moved in to steer the ball into the far corner with his left foot. Villa almost equalised when Burrows went through, but again he was dispossessed at the vital moment. Towards the end, Villa began to flag and Blues were able to hold on for a victory which was well deserved for their second half superiority.

VICTORY – NUMBER TWENTY

- 27 May 1963 – Villa Park – Crowd: 37,921
- LEAGUE CUP SEMI-FINAL SECOND LEG 0–0 – WINNING OUR FIRST MAJOR TROPHY 3–1 ON AGGREGATE
- 23 May 1963 – St Andrew's – Crowd: 31,580
- LEAGUE CUP SEMI-FINAL FIRST LEG
- WON 3–1 – scorers – Bloomfield and Leek 2

Team:
J. SCHOFIELD, S. LYNN, C. GREEN, T. HENNESSEY, T. SMITH, M. BEARD, M. HELLAWELL, J. BLOOMFIELD, J. HARRIS, K. LEEK, B. AULD

Johnny Schofield saves from Thomson whilst Smith looks on

Left: Jimmy Harris at home with his 1963 Winners Tankard. Right: Team Sheet from 23rd May 1963 programme. Below: 1963 squad with League Cup

They did things differently in 1963. There was no colour television and little sunshine so it was essential to pretend that life was good. It was the year they shot an American president, the year they deified a pop group and the year that fashion gurus devised a standard that made drainpipe trousers compulsory attire. The whole world was in transition and even football, then a means of escape for the working classes, was unsure of its role in society. Everton won the League, Manchester United the FA Cup and George Best moved from Belfast to Old Trafford. When Blues played Villa in the League Cup Final first leg at St Andrew's that May, they could not sell out the stadium. Such a scenario would be unthinkable today but in 1963, Britain was a cold place, constrained by recession and not yet ready to embrace a competition that was ignored by the top clubs. The League Cup which was won on a 3–1 aggregate, suffered from an identity crisis. Readers who shelled out three old pence for *The Birmingham Post* on Tuesday May 23 would not have been surprised to find that the report of the second leg at Villa Park was not even the most substantial story. "League Cup draw earns Blues their first major honour" went the headline but the match report by Cyril Chapman was inexplicably smaller than the article for the Kent v Warwickshire cricket match at Gravesend. Charlie Aitken was not complaining. The owner of the thickest head of hair in the game. Aitken was a young defender who, like many of his team-mates, wondered what the hell the League Cup was all about. In those days, there was no direct entry into Europe and no prize money. The two encounters in the League Cup Final are more important now than they were then. Whenever opposing fans taunt Bluenoses with chants of "you've never won f*** all" they miss the point about 1963. Schoey was baffled why the competition was deemed to be so irrelevant: "We found this strange as it had been such a big thing when Villa won it in 1961. We had a good team. Our playmaker was Jimmy Bloomfield who had been persuaded to come out of London to join us following a spell at Arsenal. He was responsible for improving the skill of Mike Hellawell who was a fast-raiding winger".

It is a mystery how Blues won but they did produce perhaps their most impressive display of the season to win the first leg 3–1 at St Andrew's in front of 31,580 people. Blues served up a treat of attacking football taking the lead through Leek in the 14th minute and controlling the game with such assurance that their supporters must have wondered why the team had performed so badly in the First Division. Villa equalised through Thomson but were no match for their opponents. Leek scored again in 52 minutes and Bloomfield made it 3–1 in the 66th minute. The second leg at Villa Park four nights later attracted 37,921 but was an anti-climax. Villa did not have the craft to stage a fight back and Blues eager to protect their lead, rather than add to it, spent most of the match kicking the ball out for throw-ins. The tactic worked and by the start of the 63–64 season Blues were able to distribute photos of their team sitting proudly on benches with the trophy in the foreground.

Gil Merrick remembers:
"We had struggled a bit in the league and the final came when the season was over. I think the rivalry between us and the Villa made it a special occasion. Our defence was very good. We had Johnny Schofield in goal, Stan Lynn and Colin Green as our full-backs. Stan, from the Villa was the best buy I ever made, He was an outstanding player and a great personality. Our half-back line consisted of Terry Hennessey, Trevor Smith and Malcolm Beard, two of whom came up through the junior ranks. The forward line included Mick Hellawell, Ken Leek, Jimmy Harris, Jimmy Bloomfield and Bertie Auld. It was a memorable victory for us. It's amazing to think that the club have not been to a major final since, but that's the way football is, isn't it? We had had a bad season and the board of Directors decided that a change was needed. It was one of those things but I was very bitter about it at the time. I had always wanted to go into management after I finished my playing career and it was even more special to do that at the club that I had actually played for for so many years. I really enjoyed it and what gave me the most satisfaction was to watch young apprentices like Terry Hennessey, Malcolm Beard, Malcolm Page and Johnny Vincent come through into the first team. We had a few players like that come through the system and I took pride in that. We won the League Cup and reached the Final of the Inter-Cities Fairs Cup in 1960 and 1961. We were the pioneers for English football in Europe."

1963 League Cup Winning Team

Surname	Appearances	Goals	Seasons
SCHOFIELD	237	0	14
LYNN	148	30	5
GREEN	217	1	9
HENNESSEY	202	3	6
SMITH	430	3	12
BEARD	403/2	32	11
HELLAWELL	213	33	8
BLOOMFIELD	147	32	4
HARRIS	115	53	4
LEEK	120	61	4
AULD	145	31	5

The 1963 League Cup Winning team, where did they go?

Surname	Outcome
SCHOFIELD	WREXHAM 1966
LYNN	STOURBRIDGE 1966
GREEN	WREXHAM 1971
HENNESSEY	NOTTINGHAM FOREST 1965
SMITH	WALSALL 1964
BEARD	ASTON VILLA 1971
HELLAWELL	SUNDERLAND 1965
BLOOMFIELD	BRENTFORD 1964
HARRIS	OLDHAM 1964
LEEK	NORTHAMPTON 1964
AULD	GLASGOW CELTIC 1965

- The second leg was held on 27 May 1963 and was a massive anti-climax with Blues' stifling Villa in a goalless draw.
- There has been much talk regarding how important the League Cup was in 1963.
- Of the 22 teams in the First Division in 1962–63 season only 11 entered the competition, those which did not enter with their final positions were:

EVERTON (1)
SPURS (2)
BURNLEY (3)
WOLVES (5)
SHEFFIELD WEDNESDAY (6)
ARSENAL (7)
LIVERPOOL (8)
NOTTINGHAM FOREST (9)
WEST BROMWICH ALBION (14)
IPSWICH (17)
MANCHESTER UNITED (19)
The sides that did enter were:
LEICESTER CITY (4)
SHEFFIELD UNITED (10)
BLACKBURN (11)
WEST HAM (12)
BLACKPOOL (13)
ASTON VILLA (15)
FULHAM (16)
BOLTON WANDERERS (18)
MANCHESTER CITY (21)
LEYTON ORIENT (22)

- Blues had finished 20th just escaping relegation

The Road to Victory

FIRST ROUND	BYE
SECOND ROUND	DONCASTER ROVERS (H) WON 5–0
THIRD ROUND	BARROW (A) DREW 1–1
THIRD ROUND REPLAY	BARROW (H) WON 5–1
FOURTH ROUND	NOTTS COUNTY (H) WON 3–2
FIFTH ROUND	MAN CITY (H) WON 6–0
SEMI FINAL FIRST LEG	BURY (H) WON 3–2
SEMI FINAL SECOND LEG	BURY (A) DREW 1–1

Match Report

Not since 1956 had Blues contested a domestic final and this was one they simply had to win, as the opposition were their neighbours and arch rivals, Aston Villa.

Villa went into the match as the bookmaker's favourites having been beaten Blues two months earlier in a League match 4–0. Both sides were at full strength in front of a first-leg St Andrew's crowd of 31,580 who were licking their lips with relish in anticipation of this Birmingham derby, which to the winner was worth much more than just "the bragging rights".

Blues started well with near misses from Jimmy Harris and Ken Leek, both of which were well saved by the Villa goalkeeper Sims. Blues had their best chance to date soon after when another shot from Harris was deflected onto the crossbar by Sims.

The competitiveness of both sides began to show when Bobby Thomson clattered Blues' 'keeper Schofield with an unnecessary late challenge for the ball and in another incident, Leek sent Crowe flying with another late tackle, both fouls coming in the early stages, as the teams "sorted each other out" in what was a typically eagerly fought out derby. There was a lot at stake! The first goal came, and for the celebrating the home fans it was scored by Leek after 14 minutes. A ball from midfield by Harris released Bertie Auld and the left wing whose cross was blasted home by Leek, this time giving Sims no chance of making a stop. Jimmy Bloomfield, with the tackles still flying in became the first casualty, leaving to have a thigh injury dealt with and he returned only to hobble on the wing so that he could to try run the knock off, this successfully did much to the relief of both the Blues' fans and Gil Merrick, the Manager. However, Villa were not beaten and got back into the game via an equaliser by Thomson. Gordon Lee started the move and after driving into Blues final third he sent in a hard, low cross which Thomson hit first time, it sped past Schofield as he was coming out to narrow the angle for the Villa man.

The second period began badly for Villa defender Sleeuwenhoek who collided with his own goalkeeper, which resulted in an injury which forced him to leave the field to receive treatment. Soon after that Blues lost their centre-half too when Trevor Smith was hurt in another rash tackle from Thomson.

The first real chance to score was taken and it restored the lead for Blues back after 52 minutes. Again Harris and Auld were the architects, and Leek the goalscorer, with a low drive in the area from Auld's pinpoint pass. The match was still bad-tempered and referee Crawford began to lose his patience with the persistent niggling fouling. Crowe became the next victim, when he was elbowed in the face after a tussle with Auld. Charlie Aitken was then given a sharp tongue-lashing when he shoved Hellawell in the chest in yet another heated exchange. Fraser and Harris came close to blows as they squared up to one another and team mates had to drag them apart. Crawford also gave them a warning as they continued to infuriate the Doncaster official. Blues finally killed the game with their third goal after 66 minutes. From a Harris right wing cross, Bloomfield dashed in unmarked (apart from the wound on his thigh) by Villa's sleeping defence to push the ball past Sims and in off the upright. Blues were leading 3–1 up, in the ascendancy and they were strolling through the rest of the game, content to take their lead to Villa Park for the second leg. In the dying moments, Sims saved Villa once again saving two excellent shots on goal from Leek then Auld. The final whistle came with Blues still holding a two goal advantage and counting the bruises from this gruelling encounter.

VICTORY – NUMBER TWENTY-ONE
- 30 March 1964 – Villa Park – Crowd: 25,890 – First Division
- WON 3–0 – scorers – Harris, Hellawell and Lynn (pen)

Team:
C. WITHERS, S. LYNN, C. GREEN, T. HENNESSEY, W. FOSTER, M. BEARD, M. HELLAWELL, J. BLOOMFIELD, J. HARRIS, K. LEEK, B. AULD

The Villa team that capitulated on that day was:
Bob Wilson, Cammie Fraser, Charlie Aitken, John Sleewenhoek, Mike Tindall, Alan Deakin, Harry Burrows, Tommy Ewing, Tony Hateley, Alan Baker and Ron Wylie.

- Today's footballers talk about fixture congestion but this victory came after playing Chelsea at home on 28 March and playing the reverse fixture against the Villa on 31 March.

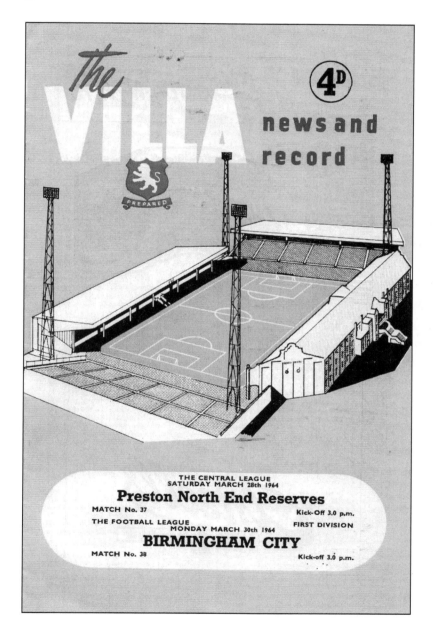

THE CENTRAL LEAGUE
SATURDAY MARCH 28th 1964

Preston North End Reserves

MATCH No. 37   Kick-Off 3.0 p.m.

THE FOOTBALL LEAGUE
MONDAY MARCH 30th 1964   FIRST DIVISION

BIRMINGHAM CITY

MATCH No. 38   Kick-off 3.0 p.m.

VICTORY – NUMBER TWENTY-TWO

- 7 October 1967 – Villa Park – Crowd: 50,067 – Second Division
- WON 4–2 – scorers – Vowden, Beard (pen) and Bridges 2

Team:

J. HERRIOT, B. MURRAY, C. GREEN, R. WYLIE, M. PAGE, M. BEARD, B. BRIDGES, J. VINCENT, F. PICKERING, G. VOWDEN, T. HOCKEY

- In Season 1967–68 Blues finished fourth in the Second Division with Villa down in 16th place.
- This was the first Second Division clash between the two teams.

Match Report

From the outset it looked like Blues were more likely to finish this clash the victors, and they did it in style. Villa's two new signings from Preston North End, Greenhalgh and Godfrey, made their presence tell and scored their two goals. Barry Stobart, a mighty presence in the side was out of the team, replaced by teenager David Rudge who was playing only his fourth senior game this season.

The crowd of 50,067 saw the Holte End play host to a mini battle, with both sets of fans struggling to be heard over each other. Villa started early on the attack, but there was no successful outcome for some fine play between Godfrey and Broadbent. Then after just four minutes Villa took the lead. Wylie misjudged his kick, and sent it directly to Anderson who crossed the ball. Greenhalgh leapt unchallenged and his header crept over the line just inside the left hand post. Herriot dropped the ball minutes later and almost gave away another goal to Villa. However, it wasn't long before Blues managed to equalise in the 21st minute. Vincent's throw in on the left went to the near post, where Vowden got his head to it and raised it for Bridges to perform the move of the game. With his back to the goal he leapt into the air and opted for a scissor-kick. He pulled it off with ease, and the ball went sailing into the net past a surprised Withers.

In the 24th minute things got very heated and resulted in a tangle between Vincent and Tindall. The referee (B.J. Homewood) managed to part then, and

Beard came over to make sure they stayed apart while they listened to their telling off. On the half-hour mark Villa's second goal came from their other new signing. Godfrey brought the ball through the Blues defence after a superb cross from Rudge and coolly slotted under Herriot. Villa's joy only lasted as long as it took for Blues to be awarded a penalty on 37 minutes. Pickering's ball went to Bridges who fed it into the centre where it hit Chatterley's boot and bounced up onto his hand. He protested furiously that it was an accident, but his pleas fell on deaf ears. Beard casually stepped up to the spot and fired the shot straight in the back of the net.

At the start of the second period Pickering's attempt was saved, and Greenhalgh also missed a chance. Then Blues took the lead when Vowden got onto a ball from Vincent and shot past Withers on 59 minutes. Just two minutes later the final goal came from Bridges who slotted in a superb cross from Wylie which had sailed over the entire Villa defence. Villa almost got one back but it wasn't to be. The only other action was a booking for Tindall in the 83rd minute for a foul on Vincent.

VICTORY – NUMBER TWENTY-THREE

- 24 February 1968 – St Andrew's – Crowd: 45,283 – Second Division
- WON 2-1 – scorers – Bridges 2

Team:
J. HERRIOT, R. MARTIN, C. GREEN, R. WYLIE, W. FOSTER, M. BEARD, B. BRIDGES, J. VINCENT, F. PICKERING, G. VOWDEN, M. PAGE

Match Report
This home win for Blues increased hopes of promotion, with 36 points out of 30 games. The match began furiously when Geoff Vowden's pass rolled perfectly into the path of Barry Bridges, who outpaced the Villa full-back Charlie Aitken and shot the ball into the net past Colin Withers after just 17 seconds of play. This was close to the league record for the fastest goal, which stood at four seconds by Bradford's Jim Fryatt in 1964. After this flying start for Blues, Villa gradually fought themselves back into the game, performances from Bobby Park and Tommy Mitchinson helping along their efforts. For a good while

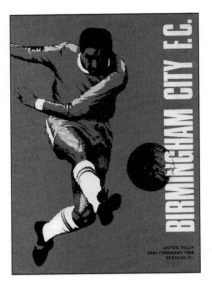

there were no more real thrills, aside from those expected from this local derby, and it was not until the 43rd minute that another goal came along.

Programme 24th February 1968

Brian Godfrey equalised for Villa after a long cross from Keith Bradley, touched down by John Woodward. The second half began and just seven minutes later Bridges was brought down in the penalty area by Aitken, but to the amazement of the huge 45,283 crowd the referee (Norman Burtenshaw) ignored the appeals from Birmingham for the clear cut penalty. After this the game was incident free until justice was done on 83 minutes. Johnny Vincent mishit a shot, but Bridges was on hand to sweep the ball into the net from a narrow angle. An attempt from Park in the final minute was saved by Jim Herriot, and the game ended with a win for Blues. It was only their third "double" over Villa, over some 36 league campaigns but few were sweeter than this one. The goals for Bridges brought his tally up to 20 in the league, nine short of Joe Bradford's club record, with a dozen games to go. The other bright spot of the game was off-the-field where officials reported no trouble between the two sets of fans before, during or after the game.

*1967/68 Team
Group*

VICTORY – NUMBER TWENTY-FOUR

21 September 1968 – St Andrew's – Crowd: 40,527 – Second Division
WON 4–0 – scorers – Vowden, Greenhoff, Vincent and Summerill

Team:
J. HERRIOT, R. MARTIN, M. PAGE, R. WYLIE, D. ROBINSON, M. BEARD,
T. HOCKEY, J. GREENHOFF, G. VOWDEN, J. VINCENT, P. SUMMERILL

- In Season 1968–69 Blues finished eighth in the Second Division with Villa in 18th place

Match Report

A re-shaped defence handed Blues their first clean sheet of the season and four blistering goals brought them an outstanding victory over rivals Villa in a dramatic Second City derby at St Andrew's. Villa who started well, paid the price for an uncoordinated final 30 minutes, when they conceded four goals. Their opponents in contract looked classy and enthusiastic throughout and fully deserved their emphatic victory.

Birmingham were put under some pressure early on and centre-half Dave Robinson was forced to make two vital clearances from off his own goalline. Robinson was just one of seven players in the Blues line-up, who were products of the clubs' youth policy.

Programme 21st September 1968

For an hour both sides seemed content on battling it out in midfield with neither prepared to take a risk and push men forward. This all changed when Birmingham suddenly sprang into action with two goals in three minutes. The first by Summerill after 63 minutes came from an assist by Greenhoff's headed knockdown, and the second three minutes later from Jimmy Greenhoff who headed home Vowden's cross. This deflated Villa who looked a despondent outfit in the closing 15 minutes. Blues were in total control and on 83 minutes scored a third when Vincent headed in from another exquisite cross by Vowden. Blues were making a mockery of the expensively assembled Villa side. Greenhoff then set up Vowden with an unmissable chance a minute from full-time to make the score a resounding 4–0. There was no doubt at all who had won and the 40,527 crowd vociferously let it be known as they left St Andrew's on a terrific afternoon for any Blues fan.

VICTORY –NUMBER TWENTY-FIVE
- 3 April 1976 – St.Andrew's – Crowd: 46,251 – First Division
- WON 3–2 – scorers – Francis, Burns and Hibbitt

Team:
D. LATCHFORD, J. CALDERWOOD, A. STYLES, H. KENDALL, J. GALLAGHER, T. WANT, G. EMMANUEL, T. FRANCIS, K. BURNS, A. NEEDHAM, T. HIBBITT
Substitute: HATTON for GALLAGHER

Match Report
Over 46,00 were inside St Andrew's that day to witness young Andy Needham miss from just six yards early on before Terry Hibbitt volleyed home a left foot effort from the edge of the box for his first Blues goal, which sent the Blues fans into raptures. Five minutes from half-time though Andy Gray equalised to send the teams in level at the break. The second half saw Kenny Burns, returning to the side after a three match ban, begin to have more and more influence with his strength upfront and on 57 minutes, a classic TF pass into his stride resulted in Kenny driving the ball past Burridge and inside the 'keeper's left-hand post to give Blues a richly deserved 2–1 advantage. It has to be said that Villa pressed forwards in their attempt to find an equaliser, but it was a dodgy penalty decision from the referee for a challenge by Joe Gallagher on Ray

Graydon that let them back in, as Graydon himself converted from the spot. There were only 15 minutes to go when that slice of luck seemed to have taken the win away from Blues but man of the match Howard Kendall crossed into the box with six minutes remaining for good old TF to flick home a delightful header that sent the Blues fans into a paroxysm of delight.

Programme 3rd April 1976

Ticket for match 3rd April 1976

VICTORY – NUMBER TWENTY-SIX

- 18 September 1976 –Villa Park – Crowd: 50,084 – First Division
- WON 2–1 – scorers – Burns and Connolly

Team:
D. LATCHFORD, M. PAGE, A. STYLES, H. KENDALL, J. GALLAGHER, T. WANT, G.K. JONES, T. FRANCIS, K. BURNS, T. HIBBITT, J. CONNOLLY
Substitute: CALDERWOOD for KENDALL

ASTON VILLA
NEWS & RECORD
OFFICIAL PROGRAMME
PRICE 15p

Programme 18th September 1976

Match Report

Villa had enjoyed a good start to the season scoring 12 goals in three home games not that we were worried as Ron Saunders was presented with the Manager of the Month award and as often is the case it proved to be followed by a defeat!

Blues were bemoaning their bad luck when in the 13th minute Chris Nicholl had sliced wildly over his own crossbar, when they broke away and Andy Gray put them in the lead. This spurred Blues on and despite the smaller numbers of Blues fans in the ground, the backing we gave the team was astonishing. Just over a quarter of an hour after they had taken the lead, TF's cross was sliced by Nicholl once more, who was having a torrid time of it and Kenny Burns nipped in to smash the ball home for the equaliser. The goal really knocked the stuffing our of our opponents and the only surprise was that it took until two minutes before half time for Blues to take the lead – and what a cracker it was too. John Connolly was fed the ball by a combination of Kendall and Burns ten yards into their half where he left Nicholl for dead, he then began cutting in from the inside-right position. He evaded tackles by Carrodus and Phillips and shot from the edge of the box, the shot going in off the 'keeper's left hand post to put Blues 2–1 ahead. After the break it seemed that Villa's only intent was to try and kick us off the park, to which they were helped by some lenient refereeing, as Phillips brought Francis down with three tackles from behind in the space of five minutes. Blues defended their lead relatively comfortably.

VICTORY – NUMBER TWENTY-SEVEN

- 10 May 1977 – St.Andrew's – Crowd: 43,721 – First Division
- WON 2–1 – scorers – Francis (pen) and Hibbitt

Team:

D. LATCHFORD, J. CALDERWOOD, G. PENDREY, M. PAGE,
J. GALLAGHER, R. SPRAGIA, G. JONES, T. FRANCIS, K. BURNS,
T. HIBBITT, J. CONNOLLY

- Two players were sent off – one from each side: Joe Gallagher and Leighton Phillips

Programme 10th May 1977

Match Report

Leighton Phillips continued his rough approach from the previous fixture and was booked for persistent fouling of Francis including two barges into his back in a short space of time. When the referee booked him, Phillips amazingly gave the referee the V-sign and a torrent of foul-mouthed abuse, then look puzzled when he was sent off. Not half an hour had transpired. That decision resulted in Andy Gray being pulled back into defence thereby removing his significant forward threat which ultimately costing the Villa the game in the last ten minutes. The terrible tackling continued Chris Nicholl was booked along with Garry Pendrey and it came as a shock to the crowd when John Deehan headed the Villa in front on 52 minutes. It took until the 76th minute for Francis to play a killer ball to Hibbitt,

holding off Gray's challenge he levelled the score, shooting wide of Burridge. After a minute or so it was 10 against 10 when Joe Gallagher trampled on John Deehan as he lay on the ground. No one argued with the decision. With a draw seemingly inevitable Francis with eight minutes to go was taken out by Gray in the penalty area, and the penalty was eventually converted by Francis.

Top: Trevor Francis scores from the penalty spot

Left: Terry Hibbitt and Trevor Francis score against the Villa

VICTORY – NUMBER TWENTY-EIGHT

- 1 October 1977 – Villa Park – Crowd: 45,436 – First Division
- WON 1–0 – scorer – Bertschin

Team:

J. MONTGOMERY, J. CALDERWOOD, G. PENDREY, A. TOWERS, P. HOWARD, T. WANT, K. BROADHURST, T. FRANCIS, K. BERTSCHIN, T. HIBBITT, G. EMMANUEL

The Villa team that capitulated on that day was:

Jimmy Rimmer, John Gidman, Leighton Phillips, Gordon Smith, John Gregory, Alex Cropley, Gordon Cowans, Dennis Mortimer, John Deehan, Brian Little (Sub: Andy Gray), Frank Carrodus.

Blues winner was a superb header from Keith Bertschin in front of the Blues fans in the bottom section of the new North Stand.

Programme 1st October 1977

Keith Bertschin scores a header whilst Gary Emmanuel looks on

VICTORY – NUMBER TWENTY-NINE

- 25 February 1978 – St Andrew's – Crowd: 33,679 – First Division
- WON 1–0 – scorer – Francis

Team:
J. MONTGOMERY, J. CALDERWOOD, A. STYLES, A. TOWERS,
J. GALLAGHER, P. HOWARD, S. FOX, T. FRANCIS, K. BERTSCHIN,
T. HIBBITT, K. DILLON
Substitute: PAGE for FOX

Programme 25th February 1978

Match Report

The club was still suffering from the impact of transfer requests from Francis and Gallagher. Jim Montgomery earned his money in this match. Some great saves from Monty and inaccurate finishing from Villa saw them hit the wood-work four times. It all came down to a goalkeeping error as just before the half hour mark. Tony Towers shot hard and low from distance, Rimmer failed to hold it and as it squirmed from his grasp Francis pounced to knock the ball over the goalline. It was backs to the wall time which resulted in some gritty defending from the Blues clearing two goal bound efforts off the line

The Villa team that capitulated on that day was:
Jimmy Rimmer, John Gidman (Sub: John Gregory), Ken McNaught, Leighton Phillips, Gordon Smith, Gordon Cowans, Tommy Craig, Dennis Mortimer, John Deehan, Brian Little, Frank Carrodus.

VICTORY – NUMBER THIRTY

- 27 December 1982 – St Andrew's – Crowd: 43,864 – First Division
- WON 3–0 – scorers – Blake, Ferguson and Handysides

Team:

T. COTON, D. LANGAN, P. VAN DEN HAUWE, B. STEVENSON, N. BLAKE, K. BROADHURST, K. DILLON, M. HARFORD, M. FERGUSON, A. CURBISHLEY, I. HANDYSIDES

- This was the game in which Blues humbled the reigning European Cup holders.

Programme 27th December 1982

Match Report

Re-produced from *THE ZULU – THE BLUENOSE BIBLE* – 16 January 2011 (I believe this was the last copy to be produced?)

"At the time Blues fans were having to suffer the taunts of Villa fans whose side were the champions of Europe, and so there was plenty of extra spice added to this game. Former Villa man Noel Blake starred in the heart of the Blues defence whose manager was Ron Saunders, the man who had walked out of Villa Park only ten months earlier after leading Blues' deadliest rivals to the league title. In front of Blues biggest crowd for five years, the St Andrew's faithful were treated to a day to remember.

Villa started the better, but with Blake and Broadhurst playing brilliantly at the heart of the Blues defence, Villa's twin threat of Gary Shaw and Peter With were subdued.

On 23 minutes Ian Handysides struck a low drive against the foot of the post. The rebound fell to Noel Blake and the ex-Villa man silenced the taunts of "reject" in the best possible way by slamming the ball into the back of the net. After the goal Villa tried to up the tempo, but Blues were more than a match with the brilliant Kevin Dillon behind all their best football. The games was a typical derby encounter with neither side having a monopoly on the ball, so the match had the feeling it could go either way. But on 70 minutes Blues struck with a vital second goal. Handysides drove a goal bound effort which Villa 'Keeper Jimmy Rimmer could only parry out. The ball fell kindly back into the path of Handysides and he sent the Blues fans wild by burying the rebound into the net with the 'keeper stranded. Villa were now a well and truly beaten side. The Blues fans roared their heroes on and their side duly obliged by going forward looking for another goal. Sure enough a third goal came when full-back Dave Langan sent a right wing cross in, which Handysides sent goalwards. Viila defender Mark Jones' clearance could only hit Blues striker Mick Ferguson and the ball bobbled past Rimmer and over the line. The game was well and truly over now. After the game Ron Saunders was seen with a rare smile on his face as he pointed out that his gutsy Blues side had stopped Villa from even creating one clear-cut chance all game. For Noel Blake the thumping victory was a day he will never forget. He described the game as one of the most memorable of his career 'I was a Blues fan as a kid' he explained 'Scoring against Villa was a marvellous feeling'"

Ian Handysides scores

VICTORY – NUMBER THIRTY-ONE

- 31 March 1984 – St Andrew's – Crowd: 23,993 – First Division
- WON 2–1 – scorers – Gayle and Stevenson

Team:

T. COTON, B. ROBERTS, J. HAGAN, N. BLAKE, M. KUHL,
B. STEVENSON, H. GAYLE, P. VAN DEN HAUWE, M. McCARRICK,
M. HALSALL, R. HOPKINS

The Villa team that capitulated on that day was:
Mervyn Day, Brendan Ormsby, Allan Evans, Colin Gibson (Sub: Des
Bremner), Gary Williams, Steve McMahon, Alan Curbishley, Paul Birch,
Mark Walters, Paul Rideout, Peter Withe(1).

Programme 31st March 1984

- The *"Match of the Day"* cameras were present at St Andrew's to catch the action. Blues took the lead from a Byron Stevenson hook shot after Villa had failed to clear a corner. Peter Withe equalised before half-time to send the teams in on level terms. Blues regained the lead early in the second half when Howard Gayle ran from the half way-line before crashing the ball past Mervyn Day into the Railway End goal.

VICTORY – NUMBER THIRTY-TWO

- 22 March 1986 – Villa Park – Crowd: 26,294 – First Division
- WON 3–0 – scorers Whitton and Clarke 2

Team:

D. SEAMAN, R. RANSON, B. ROBERTS, J. HAGAN, W. GARTON, M. KUHL, D. BREMNER, W. CLARKE, W. WRIGHT, S. WHITTON, R. HOPKINS

Programme 22nd March 1986

Match Report

John Bond had seen Villa play West Ham, and decided that Villa deserved the use of a five man defence therefore he included Billy Wright as a sweeper behind Hagan and Garton. In midfield Kuhl and Bremner were told not to let Blair and Hodge settle on the ball. The plan worked perfectly as Blues set out to take on Villa on a ground we had not even scored on since Bertschin's header back in 1977. There were early indications that Blues were going to do more than just defend as Wayne Clarke slipped Elliott as early as the 14th minute only to see his header rebound off the crossbar. Even Clarke, not the most physical of players, had got himself psyched up this game and surprisingly he was booked after 30 minutes for persistent fouling of Elliott and Allan Evans. A minute later Clarke scored the opening goal, a long clearance from Seaman was misjudged by Elliott leaving Clarke time to put his shot past Nigel Spink. Another defensive error in the 38th minute gave Blues their second goal when Evans was harried by Bremner and his resultant miskick went to Clarke who accepted the gift.

Towards the end of the first half Clarke should have completed his hattrick but after rounding Spink his shot was handled by Gary Williams from behind the line. The Blues players waited for the ref to give either a goal or a penalty but he played on much to the surprise of the Villa team. After 61 mins minutes another Villa defender lost the plot when Tony Dorigo's attempted clearance was intercepted by the head of Ray Ranson. To compound the error Williams misjudged his clearance and Spink managed to strand himself in no mans land leaving Steve Whitton an easy header into an empty net.

VICTORY – NUMBER THIRTY-THREE

- 22 August 1987 – Villa Park – Crowd: 30,870 – First Division
- WON 2–0 – scorers – Rees and Handysides

Team:
T. GODDEN, B. ROBERTS, J. DICKS, T. WILIAMS, V. OVERSON, I. HANDYSIDES, D. BREMNER, A. KENNEDY, S. WHITTON, T. REES, S. WIGLEY

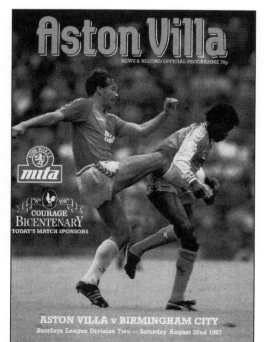

Programme 22nd August 1987

The Villa team that capitulated on that day was:
Nigel Spink, Neale Cooper, Martin Keown, Steve Sims, Kevin Gage, Bernard Gallacher, Warren Aspinall, Paul Birch, Mark Walters, Simon Stainrod (Sub: Tony Daley), Steve Hunt (Sub: David Hunt).

- This victory was the last one in the top flight until 2002 – we had to wait fifteen years for battles to re-commence.

Match Report

Blues travelled to Villa Park on the second Saturday of the season following Villa's relegation. Blues took to the pitch in an unusual white Patrick kit. It was unusual in that the kit sponsor was Matchwinner but clearly the blue home kit and grey away kits clashed with Villa's home kit which was the half claret/half blue shirt with the white vertical lines across the front.

Both goals came in the second half in front of the Blues fans in the North Stand. The first was by Tony Rees who hit a shot on the turn after Steve Whitton had headed down a cross after Villa failed to clear a corner and the second was a speculative long range shot from outside the area by Ian Handysides.

VICTORY – NUMBER THIRTY-FOUR

- 16 September 2002 – St Andrew's – Crowd: 29,505 – Premier
- WON 3–0 – scorers - Morrison, Horsfield and Enckelman (own goal)

Team:
N. VAESEN, J. KENNA, M. GRAINGER, R. SAVAGE, D. PURSE, K. CUNNINGHAM, P. DEVLIN, S. JOHN, C. MORRISON, A. CISSE, D. JOHNSON
Substitutes: G. HORSFIELD – D. POWELL – B. HUGHES

- First season in the Premier League for Blues in which we finished 13th three places above the Villa.
- Peter Enckelman was such a hero to the Blues fans due to his own goal in this game that he received a massive cheer when warming up as substitute goalkeeper when he was with Blackburn Rovers.
- This match was switched to Monday night for live Sky TV.

Match Report

It was a night for Birmingham City to cherish and one for Peter Enckelman to forget. While Birmingham coasted to a derby victory at St Andrew's, the Aston Villa goalkeeper was left to contemplate a freakish mistake that effectively sealed the match. As this was the first league derby since December 1987 and it was worth the wait. With Blues leading thanks to a first-half strike by Clinton Morrison, Enckelman allowed a throw-in by Olof Mellberg to skid under his studs and roll into the goal. It doubled the lead for Steve Bruce's men at a crucial time and paved the way for Geoff Horsfield to score a third soon after. It was an open, passionate derby and one that saw Blues rise to the occasion. Villa had their moments but, in the final analysis, crumbled when the situation demanded composure. Villa had only conceded three goals in their previous five matches but were found lacking at key moments.

Birmingham were more direct and, initially, the more confident. It was inevitable, then, that they should take the lead. In the 31st minute, Jeff Kenna hooked the ball towards the penalty spot and, with Villa's offside trap failing, Robbie Savage was able to touch the ball to Morrison whose right-footed shot from close range beat Enckelman.

Darius Vassell thought he had equalised in the 57th minute but, before his crisp volley beat Nico Vaesen, the Villa striker was flagged for offside.

The decision did not meet with the approval of Graham Taylor, the Villa manager, who, suggesting an injustice, argued long enough to earn a rebuke from David Elleray, the Middlesex-based referee who had not endeared himself to the visiting supporters. And then in the 74th minute came one of the most bizarre goals seen in 100 years at St Andrew's. Mellberg threw the ball back to Enckelman and the Villa goalkeeper inexplicably allowed the ball to bobble under his studs and trickle into the goal. There was a minute of confusion when a number of players from each side surrounded Elleray, but the conclusion was inevitable. Enckelman had unwittingly put Blues two goals ahead. From Villa's point of view, the third goal was also self-inflicted. Alpay Ozalan lost the ball close to his penalty area and allowed Horsfield – a substitute – to beat the Villa goalkeeper with a low shot from 10 yards. One had to consider the difference in the reactions of Enckelman and Horsfield to sum up the story of this surreal match.

Colin Tattum – September 16 2002

David Elleray owed Blues one for that non-penalty in the Worthington Cup Final and there is no way he could have known whether or not Peter Enckelman had touched Mellberg's throw-in before it ended up in the Villa net. He consulted the linesman and, think about it, if you were that linesman, standing by the Kop corner, with baying Blues fans behind you, were you going to say 'no goal'?

I remember Darren Purse setting the tone with an outrageous tackle on Juan-Pablo Angel that almost took off his kneecap. Elleray let play go and Villa knew that they were in for an uncomfortable night.

For so many years Blues fans had to put up with cocky and patronising comments from the claret and blue parts of the city. That night they were stunned into silence.

Programme 16th September 2002

VICTORY – NUMBER THIRTY-FIVE

- 3 March 2003 – Villa Park – Crowd: 42,602 – Premier
- WON 2–0 – scorers – Lazaridis and Horsfield – Both goals were scored at the Holte End.

Team:

N. VAESEN, J. KENNA, J. CLAPHAM, R. SAVAGE, M. UPSON, K. CUNNINGHAM, D. JOHNSON, C. DUGARRY, C. MORRISON, S. CLEMENCE, S. LAZARIDIS

Aston Villa: Enckelman, Samuel, Johnsen, Mellberg, Wright (Crouch 90) , Gudjonsson, Hendrie, Barry, Vassell, Dublin, Moore (Hadji 45) Substitutes: Hitzlsperger, Postman, Edwards.
Substitutes: G. HORSFIELD – P. DEVLIN – D. CARTER

- First double over Villa for 25 years – last time 1977–78
- During the game two Villa players were sent off, Dion Dublin for a head-butt on Blues' Robbie Savage and Joey Gudjonsson for a reckless two-footed tackle on Matthew Upson.
- Geoff Horsfield went in goal for last few minutes as Vaesen got injured and Blues had used all three substitutes.
- This game was moved to Monday night for Sky TV.
- Steve Bruce after the 2–0 win on March 3 2003; "To come here and do the double on them is a great achievement. Towards the end there was some serious provocation going on and some of the things were getting out of hand and silly. But I'm delighted with the discipline of my players. I didn't see any rash challenges from them".

Match Report

For the second time this season the Midlands derby ended disastrously for Aston Villa, who finished the game with nine men as they went down to their local rivals.

Dion Dublin and Joey Gudjonsson were sent off for the home side as Birmingham scored twice in the last 16 minutes.

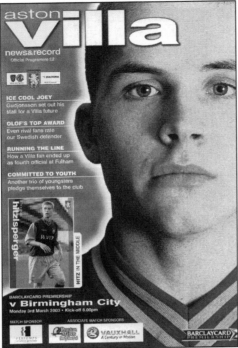

Top: Programme 3rd March 2003

Below: Corporate Team Sheet Paul Devlin signed

Goals from Stan Lazaridis and Geoff Horsfield helped the visitors move six points clear of the relegation zone.

Horsfield profited from another piece of lame goalkeeping from Peter Enckelman, who had a given away a bizarre own goal in the first meeting at St Andrew's.

As with that first meeting, this game also saw fans running on to the pitch in the closing stages as the match degenerated into farce. Dublin was dismissed five minutes into the second half. As referee Mark Halsey mulled over whether to book the Villa striker for a late tackle on Savage, Dublin then head-butted the Birmingham midfielder. Gudjonsson was red-carded for a two-footed tackle on Matthew Upson nine minutes from time.

A couple of Savage's challenges, particularly one on Gudjonsson, had set the tone for this bruising encounter. Gudjonsson and Christophe Dugarry had also clashed intermittently throughout the match and their running feud saw the Frenchman appear to spit at the Icelandic player.

Despite the feisty tackling it took 35 minutes before Halsey booked a player – showing a yellow card to Kenny Cunningham for his high tackle on Gareth Barry.

At least when the ball did occasionally reach either penalty area the tackling was more judicious. Notably when Jeff Kenna denied Barry with a last-ditch tackle, while Dublin was similarly thwarted by Jamie Clapham.

Two spectacular long-range volleys also stood out in a frenetic first half.

Lee Hendrie drove just wide of the Birmingham post, while at the other end of the pitch Peter Enckelman reacted quickly to tip a dipping effort from Dugarry over the bar.

Clinton Morrison should have also done better with a header from a Damien Johnson cross. On 74 minutes Lazaridis got on to the end of a Kenna cross to give Birmingham the lead. Soon, after Horsfield doubled Birmingham's advantage after he capitalised on Enckelman's indecision, and Gudjonsson was dismissed four minutes later.

Horsfield ended the game in goal for Birmingham after Nico Vaesen was injured clearing the ball.

VICTORY – NUMBER THIRTY-SIX
- 12 December 2004 – Villa Park – Crowd: 41,329 – Premier
- WON 2–1 – scorers – Morrison and Dunn

Team:
M. TAYLOR, O. TEBILY, S. LAZARIDIS, R. SAVAGE, M. UPSON, K. CUNNINGHAM, D. JOHNSON, C. MORRISON, E. HESKEY, D. DUNN, D. CARTER
Substitutes: J. GRAY – D. ANDERTON – J. CLAPHAM

Another howler from Villa 'keeper lets Blues score. This time it was the turn of Thomas Sorenson who let a routine Morrison shot go over his body and into the Holte End goal. The second goal was scored later in the first half from a Dunn volley following a cross from Damien Johnson.

Monday December 13 2004 *Evening Mail* reporter BILL HOWELL (*The Mail's* Mister Villa) rated BLUES in his Man for Man analysis in the match report as:

MAIK TAYLOR – DECISIVE	7
TEBILY – TROUBLED	6
LAZARIDIS – PERSISTED	7
CUNNINGHAM – FOCUSSED	8
UPSON – COLOSSAL	9
JOHNSON – TIGERISH	8
SAVAGE – INSPIRATIONAL	8
CARTER – COMBATIVE	8
DUNN – ELUSIVE AT FIRST	7
MORRISON – EXCELLENT	8
HESKEY – POWERHOUSE	8

Martin Rogers in *The Daily Mirror* 13 December 2004 headlined the game as "JINXED VILLA SORE LOSERS".

"Once again Aston Villa suffered a heavy dose of misery at the hands of their most hated rivals – and the repercussion could keep rumbling on. Villa failed to get the better of Birmingham for the fifth match in a row. It's a run that is quickly turning into a jinx.

In the past three seasons the Villa careers of Graham Taylor, Alpay, Peter Enckelman and Dion Dublin were dealt irreparable damage by derby setbacks and this contest offered no relief.

Two years on from Peter Enckelman, Thomas Sorensen produced another goalkeeping gaffe to hand Clinton Morrison the opener and from there on there was no way back for the home side."

Match Report

Birmingham continued their good run of form against Aston Villa with a 2–1 win in the Midlands derby

First half goals from Clinton Morrison and David Dunn were enough to give Steve Bruce's men their first win in five games and inflict a first home defeat of the season on Villa although they were given a late scare when Gareth Barry pulled a goal back in the dying seconds.

Birmingham came out of the traps flying and Matthew Upson sent a header from Robbie Savage's free kick just over the crossbar after two minutes.

The visitors were gifted the lead on nine minutes when Morrison found the net after a terrible blunder by Thomas Sorensen.

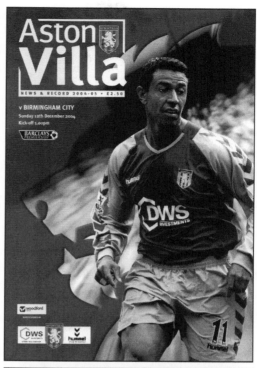

Top: Programme 12th December 2004

Below: Corporate Team Sheet

Emile Heskey flicked the ball into the path of Morrison who turned and hit a first time shot goalwards which Sorensen inexplicably let bounce over him and into the net.

Villa tried to fight their way back into the contest, but struggled to create any clear goal scoring opportunities with Gavin McCann flashing a shot wildly over the crossbar. Birmingham doubled their advantage on 19 minutes with Dunn firing home

Squadcheck   **Aston Villa**
                                                      Football Club

ASTON VILLA V BIRMINGHAM CITY
SUNDAY 12 DECEMBER 2004 - KICK-OFF 1.00PM

1.	Thomas Sorensen	1.	Maik Taylor
2.	Mark Delaney	2.	Olivier Tebily
3.	Jlloyd Samuel	4.	Kenny Cunningham ©
4.	Olof Mellberg ©	5.	Matthew Upson
6.	Gareth Barry	8.	Robbie Savage
8.	Gavin McCann	10.	David Dunn
9.	Juan Pablo Angel	11.	Stan Lazaridis
11.	Nolberto Solano	16.	Emile Heskey
15.	Ulises De La Cruz	19.	Clinton Morrison
18.	Carlton Cole	22.	Damien Johnson
24.	Steven Davis	24.	Darren Carter
13.	Stefan Postma (GK)	3.	Jamie Clapham
16.	Mathieu Berson	18.	Nico Vaesen (GK)
17.	Peter Whittingham	21.	Julian Gray
19.	Liam Ridgewell	32.	Darren Anderton
22.	Luke Moore	33.	Dwight Yorke

Managers

David O'Leary   Steve Bruce

Officials

Referee: Mr S Dunn
Assistant Referees: Mr A J Green & Mr P Sharp
Fourth Official: Mr H Webb

past Sorensen after more slack Villa defending. Morrison sent Damien Johnson clear down the right who easily outpace Jlloyd Samuel and the Northern Ireland International picked out Dunn inside the box to sweep his shot into the net.

Villa's defence was at sixes and sevens and Dunn came close to adding a third goal on 24 minutes after being played in on goal by Heskey, but Sorensen spread himself well to save the midfielder's shot with his legs. Dunn had another good chance six minutes later after a clever one-two with Heskey gave him a sight of goal, but he dragged his left-foot shot well wide of the target.

The game threatened to boil over on 36 minutes as a number of players got involved in a scuffle after Johnson appeared to kick out at Gareth Barry and when calm was finally restored Johnson was booked by referee Steve Dunn. Blues were inches away from grabbing a third goal two minutes before the break when Dunn sent Heskey scampering clear on the left and he worked his way past Olof Mellberg and was unlucky to see his shot rebound of the post.

Villa must have come out for the second half with the criticism of David O'Leary still ringing in their ears and Carlton Cole had their first shot on target a minute after the break with a volley from Barry's knock-down going straight at Maik Taylor. Barry had a half-chance to pull a goal back for Villa on 57 minutes when Solano and De La Cruz combined down the right with the full-back sending over a dangerous centre which the versatile midfielder could not direct on target. Barry had the ball in the net on 66 minutes from Solano's free-kick, but his effort was ruled out for handball and the midfielder was booked for the offence.

Villa continued to pour forward and they had claims for a penalty turned down 13 minutes from time when Juan Pablo Angel's shot appeared to strike the arm of Olivier Tebily, but Dunn waved away their appeals. Villa gave themselves a lifeline in injury time with Barry getting on the end of Mellberg's long pass and rifling a shot past Taylor to set up a frantic finale, but Blues held on to take the bragging honours

VICTORY – NUMBER THIRTY-SEVEN

- 20 March 2005 – St Andrew's – Crowd: 29,382 – Premier
- WON 2–0 – scorers – Heskey and Gray

Team:

M. TAYLOR, M. MELCHIOT, J. CLAPHAM, D. CARTER, M. UPSON,
K. CUNNINGHAM, D. JOHNSON, W. PANDIANI, E. HESKEY,
S. CLEMENCE, S. LAZARIDIS
Substitutes: M. NAFTI – J. GRAY – C. MORRISON

Match Report

Goalkeeping howler nets Blues a win in second city derby. Where have we heard that before? Thomas Sorensen handed Blues three points on a plate for the second time this season, letting Emile Heskey's 53 minute strike squirm under his body. Julian Gray scored his second goal for Blues to seal three points. Blues were the better side for long periods and although it wasn't pretty, who cares? Walter Pandiani fired a volley wide early on; Darren Carter's rasping drive fizzed passed the post and a powerful run and cross from Emile only needed a touch. Villa's only chance of the first half just before the break from a Norbert Solano free-kick, which Maik Taylor at full stretch brilliantly tipped onto the post. Blues broke the deadlock when Emile shrugged off Martin Laursen and Olof Mellberg and fired home under the body of the embarrassed Sorensen. Walter's towering header brought a fine save from Sorensen before some dire Villa defending allowed Julian Gray a clear run on goal to add a second. A superb double save from Taylor late on prevented any last minute worries.

Melchiot's show boating at the end was priceless particularly as Hendrie's exception to it resulted in him getting booked.

Programme 20th March 2005

VICTORY – NUMBER THIRTY-EIGHT

- 1 December 2010 – St Andrew's – Crowd: 27,679 – League Cup
- WON 2–1 – scorers – Larsson (pen) and Zigic

Team: (With ratings from *Birmingham Mail*, Thursday 2 December 2010

- BEN FOSTER 7: *Powerless to prevent goal. Made a couple of routine saves from Bannan and a decent stop from Ireland.*
- STEPHEN CARR 7: *Typically combative. Cautioned for chopping down Warnock. Started the move for Blues' winner with smart pass.*
- LEE BOWYER 6: *Won penalty for opener, lost Agbonlahor for equaliser. Departed early with apparent knock.*
- ROGER JOHNSON 7: *As ever provided a solid layer of protection with blocks and headers and kept it together as Villa dominated the second half.*
- LIAM RIDGEWELL 6: *Did his job at the back and got forward when he could. Worked as hard as anyone for first win against his old club.*
- SEB LARSSON 6: *Kept his composure to beat Friedel from the spot. Steady enough but failed to trouble Villa enough from deadballs and open play.*
- CAMERON JEROME 8: *Star Man – Willing runner, kept Villa on their toes. Wasted a gilt edged one-on-one first half. But provided the killer ball for the winner.*
- BARRY FERGUSON 7: *His usual steady and composed self. Used the ball well despite younger opponents nipping at his heels.*
- SCOTT DANN 7: *Booked for foul on Agbonlahor. Made a crucial goalline block to deny Young. Pretty solid throughout,*
- KEITH FAHEY 6: *Former Villa youngster did not see enough of the ball to test Young. Involved a bit more after the break.*
- NIKOLA ZIGIC 7: *Grabbed a dramatic winner after controversy over whether his first-half "goal" should have stood.*
- SUBSTITUTES: DAVID MURPHY: *After 87 minutes for Larsson.* CRAIG GARDNER: *After 65 minutes for Bowyer. Whizzed a cracking strike just wide.* MATT DERBYSHIRE: *After 90 minutes for Zigic.*
- Not Used: MAIK TAYLOR – MICHEL – JEAN BEAUSEJOUR – MARTIN JIRANEK

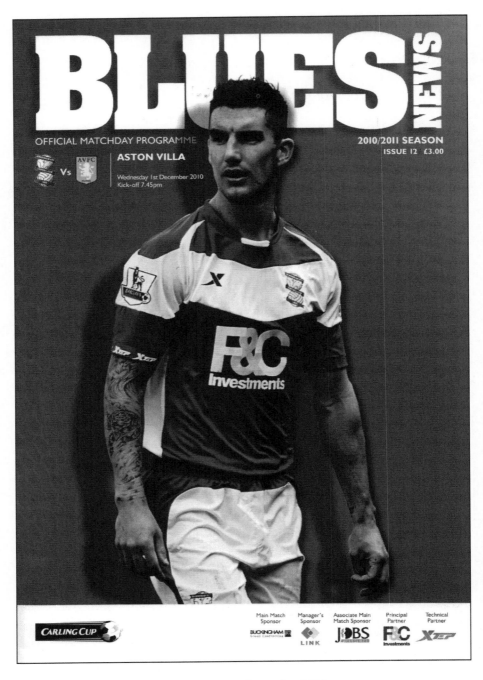

Programme 1st December 2010

Tickey for match on 1st December 2010

That Birmingham City and Aston Villa have long been opposites probably couldn't be made more evident by the events of 1 December 2010. In a Carling Cup quarter-final clash at St Andrew's, the two sides from England's second city battled throughout the night, with City's Nikola Zigic seeing his shot deflected into goal with six minutes remaining, for a 2–1 Blues win. That Birmingham, ironically very much the second club in the second city for which it's named, had claimed victory over Villa for the first time in more than five years wasn't what epitomised the enmity between the clubs; it was what happened after the official blew time and the players left the pitch.

At that point, the Blues supporters from the Tilton Road stand took to the pitch and advanced until they met a police cordon in front of the opposite goal, quickly formed to protect their target, the visiting Villa fans in the Railway Stand. The Birmingham mob did not attempt to break through the constabulary. Instead, they went over them, releasing a fusillade of flares, bottle rockets and just plain bottles. The Claret and Blue enemy hadn't come quite so prepared, so they defended their honour with what was at hand. Much like watching a volleyball match from under the net, the police craned their necks, heads swivelling from under raised shields, as they watched pyrotechnics sail in one direction and chair backs and seats fly in the other, content to wait until both sides had run out of ammunition before making any arrests.

While such riots, which were once commonplace at one point in English football, as well as the rest of Europe, have become a rare occurrence, this was the second such clash between the two groups of supporters at St Andrew's in the same calendar year.

This was the first mid-week game between the two sides since 2003 and violence between the two sets of supporters and hooligan firms occurred in the second of the two games after we had beaten them 2–1. Blues supporters ran onto the pitch and confronted the away fans, this result in mayhem with flares being set off (who in their right mind goes to a football match armed with a flare), seats were ripped out and missiles hurled.

The fracas was as always fuelled by alcohol and an attack on a Bluenose pub came as no surprise in what was acknowledged as being a warzone.

As the home club Blues were fined £40,000 by the Football Association for "failing to control their fans" however it was unlikely that it was Bluenoses that ripped apart the toilet facilities in the away fans area!

Seven people were arrested and 27 injured during the madness even though 500 police officers (five times the usual police presence) were on duty.

Match Report

"ZIGIC IN THE NIK OF TIME"

But Blues passage to semis wrecked by pitch invasion.

By Gregg Evans

Nikola Zigic was the hero as his 84th-minute goal secured Blues a Carling Cup semi-final against West Ham United at the expense of bitter rivals Villa.

His winner sparked wild celebrations and ugly scenes following a pitch invasion at St Andrew's as a fiercely contested Second City derby ended in chaos.

Both sets of fans threw missiles at each other, including flares, before order was restored.

Young Villa midfielder Jonathan Hogg had come in for veteran Robert Piries while Gabby Agbonlahor replaced John Carew upfront. Both Piries and Carew were relegated to the bench. For Blues, Zigic replaced the injured Alexander Helb as the hosts started with a 4-4-2 formation as they sought to claim the bragging rights for the first time in eight games

Both sides looked nervous in the early exchanges as the two sets of fans rallied their troops. It was a special atmosphere – one that could only be generated from a game of this importance. And it was the home crowd who were jumping for joy after just 12 minutes. As Villa's defence struggled to clear their lines, Cameron Jerome battled to win the ball in the box. He squared it to Lee Bowyer but a rash tackle from Richard Dunne sent the former England international tumbling. Referee Chris Foy pointed straight to the spot and Sebastian Larsson placed the ball down in front of Villa's travelling support. His spot-kick wasn't the greatest penalty but it sent Brad Friedel the wrong way, and St Andrew's went absolutely crazy. Villa were in trouble and had the difficult task of breaking down a Blues side well known for their ability to hold on to slender advantages.

The visitors tried desperately to get at the home side's backline but they were struggling to produce the kind of killer ball that Agbonlahor was craving. On 26 minutes Blues could have doubled their lead had it not been for an excellent last-ditch tackled by Luke Young. Larsson fed Zigic and the Serbian looked certain to score from eight yards out but Young intercepted. The giant striker was again in the thick of the action as he had a goal ruled out for offside.

Corporate Team Sheet

The ball only just crossed the line and there was some confusion why the goal had been disallowed but it was because Scott Dann was impeding Friedel in between the sticks. Blues were cursing the decision and had further reason to grumble as Villa levelled the scores a minute later. Agbonlahor went up the other end and grabbed the equalised with a fine finish past Ben Foster. Hogg fed the influential striker and he turned Bowyer to score at St Andrew's for the third successive game.

Agbonlahor received endless taunts from the home crowd throughout the game and even had snowballs pelted at him and his team-mates as they celebrated, but the forward was happy to do his talking on the pitch. It was rapidly turning into an exciting cup tie and when Zigic put Jerome clean through his cheeky dink went inches wide on 33 minutes. It was a gilt-edged chance but one that sparked the home side into life again, although they failed to test Friedel.

At the other end Barry Bannan, celebrating his 21st birthday, had a feeble effort on goal that was easily dealt with by Foster.

With the game in the balance at the break both sides came out with renewed vigour. Blues were backed by the vociferous Tilton Road End and Villa attacked their equally-as-loud posse located in the Railway End. Within 30 seconds there was a chance at either end but both 'keepers were alert to the danger. Keith Fahey danced past Luke Young and crossed for Jerome but Friedel was the quickest to react. The American bowled it out to Ashley Young who then dazzled his way past the Blues backline before crossing for Agbonlahor but again it was the 'keeper who came out on top – Foster ending the danger. Despite it being a bitterly-contested game, Stephen Carr was the first name in the book on 66 minutes for a foul on Stephen Warnock. Craig Gardner was then introduced to the fray as his old club were beginning to get on top. He was nearly gifted the perfect opportunity to hurt his former employees when Dunne slipped and let Blues in, but his 20-yard effort went sailing wide.

Dann then blocked Young's attempt but Blues turned the screw and grabbed a late winner. Zigic was the hero as he scrambled in Jerome's cross, despite Luke Young's last-ditch tackle to send the ground into eruptions and Alex McLeish's men through to the semi-finals.

"CROSSING THE DIVIDE – THE PLAYERS"

Once upon a time there was a Bluenose who was good enough to sign a professional football contract with his beloved Birmingham City, after a successful career he is then offered a transfer to Aston Villa. What does he do?

I am sure that all of the Bluenoses reading this book who might have been good enough at football to be put in that position would refuse the offer outright without any consideration of earning better money or extending their career.

That however was a fairy tale because there is no shortage of players who have appeared for both clubs.

Notable players who have been transferred directly between the clubs are listed below.

- Villa legend Harry Hampton transferred to Blues after the First World War and helped the club to the Second Division title. Striker Hampton had 16 years at Villa scoring 215 goals in 341 games (63%), during his two year stay at Blues he bagged 31 goals in 57 games 54%.
- The last established first-team player to make the move from Villa to Blues was Des Bremner in 1984.
- The most recent permanent transfer from Aston Villa to Birmingham City was that of Craig Gardner during the 2009–10 season. A self-proclaimed Bluenose played 80 times for Villa scoring six goals in the period 2005 to 2010 His one season stay at Blues generated nine goals in 42 appearances (See "Kissing The Badge").
- The last player to move directly in the other direction was Chris Sutton in 2006/07. Chris Sutton was on loan from Glasgow Celtic scoring once in 10 games finishing the season at Villa Park where he scored once in 8 games. What a striker!
- The winger Charlie Athersmith played for Villa 269 times between 1891 and 1901 scoring 75 goals he moved to Blues and in the period 1901 to

1905 scored 12 times in 100 appearances.

- Walter Corbett played for Blues during the period 1907 to 1911 playing 48 games after joining Villa in 1904.
- Frederick Chapple (Inside-forward) scored three goals in nine Villa games from 1906–1908 before moving to Blues where he made 51 appearances scoring 15 times in a two season stay.
- Goalscoring full-back Stan Lynn scored 26 times for Blues in 131 matches between 1961 and 1966, prior to that in an eleven year spell at Villla Park he scored 36 in 281 games.
- Bobby Thomson who also played for Wolverhampton Wanderers scored 56 in 140 for the Villa between 1959–63 before switching to St Andrew's where he scored 26 times in 131 matches.
- Ron Wylie played inside-forward and wing-half for Villa in 196 games scoring 16 times. He switched to Blues in 1965 after seven years at Villa and went onto to make 128 appearance during 1965–70 scoring twice.
- Dutch born John Sleeuwenhoek was a centre-half who had 226 appearances for Villa between 1961–1967 scoring a solitary goal, he moved across the city playing only 30 games for Blues through to 1970.
- Defender Noel Blake never made the grade as a defender at Villa Park making only four appearances in 1979 to 1982 he had two seasons at St Andrew's scoring five times in 76 games.
- Bluenose Robert "Hoppy" Hopkins had a three match career at Villa scoring a single goal during 1979–1983 he moved to his beloved Blues and scored 20 goals from midfield in 123 games during the period 1983–86 before moving to West Bromwich Albion.
- Des Bremner had two very similar careers with both the Blues and the Villa during 1978 to 1984 he played 174 games scoring nine from midfield whilst a five year stay at Blues resulted in five goals from 168 appearances.
- Defender Liam Ridgewell was at Villa from 2001 to 2007 scoring seven times in 79 matches he played 139 times for the Blues scoring nine goals before moving to West Bromwich Albion in 2012. His move in the Summer of 2007 was the first direct move from Villa Park to St Andrew's since Des Bremner in 1984. Steve Bruce was quoted, "Liam is not fright-

ened by the situation or by the challenge its presents. He has shown some courage moving from across the city and I'm sure he'll handle it very well. He wants to play, he wants to train, he loves the game and you can see that. He's young, he's left hand sided, good in the air and aggressive and he's got all the ingredients to be a big success at Birmingham and I'm sure he will be. I also believe the supporter of Birmingham will recognise he is a good player and will treat him with all the respect he deserves."

- Curtis Davies having already played for West Bromwich Albion joined Villa in 2008 and made 37 appearances in his three year stay scoring two goals to date he has played 48 times for the Blues scoring five times before joining Hull City prior to the start of the 2013–14 season.

- Freddie "Diamond" Wheldon was the first player to play for all three Birmingham teams – Blues, Villa and West Bromwich Albion back at the end of the 1890s. His other claims to fame were that he scored Blues' first ever goal in the Football League and also scored our first-ever penalty in October 1894 against Villa!

- Dennis Mortimer – regarded by Villa fans as one of their greatest ever players – also played for Birmingham City in the 1986–7 season. Dennis recalls, "I did wonder how the fans would react to me playing for Blues given my links to Villa. Indeed on the first home game of the season against Bradford, the announcement of my name on the team sheet was greeted with boos from some sections of the crowd. However I think I endeared myself to the fans though, as we won the game 2–1 and I scored both goals".

- Kevin Phillips played for Villa in the 2005–06 season before moving to Blues in 2008 via West Bromwich Albion.

- Geoff Vowden scored 79 times in a 221 match career with Blues from 1964–1971 in a three season period with Villa he scored 22 in 97.

- Midfielder Alan Curbishley was with the Blues from 1979 to 1983 making 130 appearances in which he scored 11 times he had one season at Villa Park scoring once in 36 games.

- Noel Blake holds a unique place in the city's football history being the first black player to play for both Blues and Villa.

- In the 1900s Billy George made 399 appearances for Villa before joining

Blues as a coach and making his one and only appearance after being called on following an injury to regular goalkeeper Horace Bailey. At the grand old age of 37, he is still the oldest player to make his debut for Blues.

- Sam Smith scored two goals against the Villa at Villa Park on his debut on 16 November 1931.

blue-villain

THEY PLAYED FOR BOTH TEAMS

Dennis Mortimer, one of an elite group of footballers who has lifted the European Cup, spoke to James Iles about leading Aston Villa to the heights of domestic football in the early 1980s and his season spent, in less fruitful times, at Birmingham City.

Dennis was born in Liverpool in April 1952 though after starting out with Kirby Boys, he spent most of his playing career in the Midlands beginning at Coventry City where he turned professional in 1969.

Six years, 215 appearances and ten goals later, Ron Saunders signed Dennis, an excellent midfield player with determination and drive, and brought him to Villa Park paying £175,000 in December 1975.

He quickly became a key player in the Villa midfield as they marched to victory in the League Cup Final of 1977, beating Everton 3-2 after extra time.

And as captain he famously led Villa firstly to the Football League Championship title in 1981 and then to the 1982 European Cup final in Rotterdam where a Peter Withe goal defeated Bayern Munich 1-0.

He also lifted the Super Cup the same year after a 3-1 aggregate win over Barcelona thus immortalising himself in the claret and blue half of the city.

Dennis said: "The greatest days of any player's career are when they are winning trophies and I had the greatest time of my life at Aston Villa.

"We won the league championship with a squad of 14 players and I was one of seven players who played every match in that season.

"There was no squad system like we see today which I think is a smokescreen for players to hide behind."

And Dennis, a boyhood Liverpool supporter, has some sweet memories from the title winning season.

"We knew we had to break the mould to win the league by beating the dominant teams and two games stand out - when we beat

Liverpool 2-0 at home and I scored and beating Everton 3-1 away when I also scored - which was extra special to score a goal on Merseyside."

After totalling 36 goals in 406 games for Villa, he moved on to Brighton and Hove Albion though he did not spend so long on the south coast as he had not made a permanent move down from the Midlands.

Dennis, who has lived in Lichfield for the past 20 years with his wife Jan with whom he has two sons, aged 21 and 18, admits he had doubts over his next move - to the Blues - especially given his near iconic status at Aston Villa.

"I almost went to Wolves on loan as Brian Little was caretaker manager but it fell through. Then when John Bond came in for me I had little choice other than to move to Blues as I wanted a transfer to a Midlands club and they were the only ones in the area who were interested."

John Bond, manager during Blues' 1986-87 season, fielded a decent footballing side, featuring Wayne Clarke, Dennis's fellow ex-Villain Des Bremner, Steve Whitton and Julian Dicks, which started the

campaign well but soon fell foul of the club's financial problems of the time.

"I did wonder how the fans would react to me playing for Blues given my links to Villa," said Dennis. Indeed, on the first home game of the season, against Bradford, the announcement of his name on the team sheet was met with boos from some sections of the crowd.

"I think I endeared myself to the fans though as we won the game 2-0 - and I scored both goals," he added.

Blues had got off to a good start to the season, winning their first two games and were sitting pretty in the top six.

"But some players had a loss of form and that coupled with us having to sell players like Wayne Clarke, we lost firepower up front and just about managed to stay up by the end of the season," said Dennis.

"I enjoyed my time at Blues though. It was first team football, they were a talented side and with a bit of money they might have done better if they didn't have to sell players to survive."

Dennis is still involved with football today as a regional coach for the PFA, working with trainees, scholars and academy players all over the Midlands.

And he had this to say of the Blues and Villa teams who'll line up for their first top flight derby in 16 years tonight at St. Andrew's.

"I watched Blues beat Leeds 2-1 the other week and I was impressed. They've started really well and as long as they don't pick up any injuries to key players I think they will be okay," he said.

"Graham Taylor is rebuilding the Villa side, he's trying to change things round and has brought some good young players in. It's a transitional period for the club.

"I think tonight's result will be governed by who is more up for it which will probably be the Blues players but I think it will be a close game."

Dennis Mortimer shows off the League Championship trophy to the Villa Park faithful.

Mortimer in action for Blues during his brief spell at St. Andrew's.

Others include

CHARLES HARE (Villa 1891–95, Blues 1896–98).

ROWLAND HARPER (Blues 1905–07, Villa 1907–08).

CHARLES MILLINGTON (Villa 1905–08, Blues 190912).

FRED CHAPPLE (Villa 1906–08, Blues 1908–10).

KEN TEWKESBURY (Blues 1929–32, Villa 1932–33).

CHARLES PHILLIPS (Villa 1935–37, Blues 1937–39).

JOCK MULRANEY (Blues 1946–47, Villa 1948–49).

TREVOR HOCKEY (Blues 1965–71, Villa 1973–74).

BRUCE RIOCH (Villa 196–74 Blues, 1978–79).

FRANK CARRODUS (Villa 1974–79, Blues 1982–83).

DAVID GEDDIS (Villa 1979–83, Blues 1984–87).

MARK JONES (Villa 1981–84, Blues 1984–87).

LEE JENKINS (Villa 1978–80, Blues 1985–86).

PHIL ROBINSON (Villa 1986–87, Blues 1990–91).

LES SEALEY (Villa 1991–92, Blues 1992–93).

CARL TILER (Villa 1995–97, Blues 2000–2001).

MALCOLM BEARD (Blues 1960–71, Villa 197–73).

WILL DEVEY (Villa 1892–94, Blues 1898–99).

ALEC LEAKE (Blues 1895–1902, Villa 1902–08).

ALEX McCLURE (Blues 1911–24, Villa 1924–25).

MARTIN THOMAS (Loan).

FRED WHELDON (Blues 1892–96, Villa 1896–1900).

FRANCIS CORNAN (Blues 1905–08, Villa 1908–09).

ALAN CURBISHLEY (Blues 1979–83, Villa 1983–85).

EDMUND EYRE (Blues 1906–09, Villa 1908–11, Blues 1913–15).

CAMMIE FRASER (Villa 1962–64, Blues 1964–66).

JACK HIGGINS (Villa 1907, Blues 1908).

DENNIS HODGETTS (Villa 1888–96, Blues 1896–97).

FRED KERNS (Blues 1905–09, Villa 1908–12). (JOHN KEARNS?)

ALBERT LINDON (Blues 1910–11, Villa 1911–12).

RAY MARTIN (Villa 1960–61, Blues 1962–1976.)

TONY MORLEY (Villa 1979–84, Blues 1984–85).

JIM MURRAY (Villa 1900–02, Blues 1901–02).

ARTHUR PHOENIX (Blues 1923–24, Villa 1924–25).

TONY REES (Villa 1983-84, Blues 1983-88).

KEVIN ROGERS (Villa 1983, Blues 1984).

BRYAN SMALL (Villa 1991–95, Blues 1994–95).

GEORGE TRAVERS (Blues 1907–09, Villa 1908–09).

ARCHIE VALE (Blues 1882, Villa 1883).

COLIN WITHERS (Blues 1960–65, Villa 1964–1969).

JACK WILCOX (Villa 1907–09, Blues 1908–11).

DWIGHT YORKE (Villa 1989–98, Blues 2004–05).

PETER WITHE (Blues 1975–77, Villa 1980–85, Blues 1987–88).

EMILE HESKEY (Blues 2004–2006, Villa 2008–12).

KEVIN POOLE (Villa 1984–87, Blues 1997–2001).

GARY CHARLES (Villa 1994–99, Blues 2000–01).

TONY HATELEY (Villa 1963–67, Blues 1969–71).

WARTIME GUEST PLAYERS

Villa players that appeared for Blues during the World War conflicts.

1915–1919; WORLD WAR ONE

HAROLD EDGLEY

CHARLIE WALLACE

TOM WESTON

1939–46; WORLD WAR TWO

JIMMY ALLEN

FRANK BROOME

GEORGE CUMMINGS

GEORGE EDWARDS

BOB IVERSON

ALEX MASSIE

FRANK MOSS

KISSING THE BADGE

I think we Bluenoses can just about accept players joining from the Villa as long as they give 100% for the badge. Football is no longer about 11 Brummies pulling on the Royal Blue shirt, it is big business and on the assumption that Curtis Davies never asked for a transfer his moves from West Bromwich Albion to Aston Villa (£8m), Villa to Blues (£3.5m) and in the close season prior to 2013–14 joining Hull City from Blues for £2.25m at 10% "signing on" fee will have netted him £1,375,000. Not bad for a former England Under-21 international who spent time on loan at Leicester City.

However what does seriously irritate fans is when players moving from rival clubs suddenly declare their undying devotion to the club that they have supposedly supported all their life. The Blues version of Robbie Keane was Craig Gardner.

On 27 January 2010 the headlines on the back page of *The Birmingham Mail* announced "I WON'T LET YOU DOWN" Colin Tattum's article included a quote from Gardner, "People say when you become a footballer it's a dream come true but when you sign for the club you support, what more can you ask for? You just pinch yourself. I don't think I've had more than three hours sleep this week. I've been on to my agent all the time asking 'is it done, is it done?' and in the end he just told me to relax. I just can't wait to put that blue and white shirt on, score some goals and help Birmingham City pick up points. There's pressure on me. They've invested money in me and I've got to respond. There's a responsibility on my shoulders now. I was just the boy who came through the ranks – now I'm the man Blues have paid £3.5milliion for. I want to prove why I am worth that money to the fans, why the chairman has paid that money and why the manager wanted me. I won't let them down, I won't let anybody down."

Gardner, Yardley-born said it was Blues or nothing when his future at Villa became clouded. "I said to the gaffer (Martin O'Neill) that if I'm moving. I want to go to Blues. Even if there were other teams interested. I'd rather stay but if Blues came in I asked him to please let me know. He said 'Craig, we'll sort it out'. Fortunately Blues did come in and now I'm here and signed my life away. I love it" As for his allegiance, Gardner said he was Blues through and through. "Having played for the Villa, everyone thinks I'm a Villa fan but I'm a Bluenose. I have been all my life. I was a mascot at John Frain's testimonial. But I don't have to prove anything to anyone. People who know me, my close friends and family, they all know I'm a Blues fan. As they say, once a Blue always a Blue".

Compare this article to one which appeared in *The Sunday Mercury* on 15 April 2007 written by Mat Kendrick.

"Boyhood Holte-ender Craig Gardner first set his sights on becoming a claret and blue legend when he ran on to the Villa Park pitch as a seven-year old trespasser during the 1994 League Cup semi-final against Tranmere Rovers. 'I signed for Villa when I was 15 and since then these have been the best days of my life. I'm a Villa fan. I've come through the ranks and nothing can be better.' And the Solihull-based midfielder who rejected the chance to join Blues four years ago has made it his mission to achieve legendary status in the eyes of the Villa Park public. 'I love everything about the Villa and I want to stay here and be a legend – that's my aim.'"

Bearing this in mind it is little wonder that Bluenoses took little notice of his words and great offence at his actions, when as soon as Blues lost its Premier League status Gardner moved to Sunderland in June 2011. He was the first out of the door and left the fans with these words: "The last 18 months have been the best 18 months of my playing career so far … It really hurts when I hear anyone question my loyalty or how much Blues means to me … I will always be grateful to the Blues and the club will always have a special place in my heart."

One can only imagine his Sunderland press conference going something like this:

"I am delighted to be joining my boyhood heroes Sunderland, for years as a young player at Aston Villa and Birmingham City I yearned for the chance to pull on the red and white stripes. As a regular visitor to Roker Park (once in a blue moon) I am glad to have the chance to realise my dream of playing at The Stadium of Light (until a better offer comes around or you are relegated)".

I think this supporter sums it up:

"He was the kid who came in from our hated rivals to declare he'd always been a bluenose. Pictures of him at John Frain's testimonial circulated, and he became a regular fixture in the Birmingham central midfield, top scoring for Blues last season. However, apparently playing for his boyhood heroes isn't enough for Craig Gardner; the word is he wants to stay in the Premiership. The problem with kissing the badge when you score is that if your team goes through a rough patch and gets relegated, you begin to look a bit of a superficial mug if you decide you want to move on. Take Alan Smith for example; he swore on *Soccer AM* he'd never play for Leeds United's hated rivals … yet guess where he ended up. Okay, there were mitigating factors, but I don't believe the fans forgave him so easily for it. I'm not saying for one minute that I expect all players to be one hundred percent loyal to their clubs; but it does stick in the craw that a player who said the only club he wanted to sign for was us, now wants to move on because the going got tough. It's a shame really. Whilst I was prepared to see us lose quite a few players, Gardner was one of three I really wanted us to keep, to build a team around. I was convinced that in the Championship Craig Gardner would set the division aflame; if he could get nine goals in the Premiership then I reckoned he could be on for fifteen to twenty in the second tier. With a more dynamic, youthful team around him, I thought Blues could rebuild and get promoted, and allow themselves a better stab at staying up the next time. I was sure that as a Bluenose who's career had come on leaps and bounds whilst with us, he'd stick with us and get us back up. Yet after listening to his interview with Tom Ross, like many Blues fans I became disillusioned; he didn't once mention his Blues roots and implied his exit was imminent. It's true we'll get far more than the £3million or so we paid for him – a figure of £8 million was mooted by James Nursey of the *Daily Mirror*, but once again a player who probably could have become a legend has kicked us in the nuts because he was worried how a season in the second tier would affect his credibility; not to mention his bank balance. One thing McLeish leaving has done is to harden me to the thought that Blues will lose most of their more saleable assets. Whilst it hurts to see players go, that could and probably should have been good for the club, I can't help but think that these are the players who got us relegated in the first place. There is an argument that if Gardner had kept to his feet in the game against Wolves, we might not have gone down at all. As football has got more cynical, I can't help but wonder that if Gardner rocks up somewhere like Newcastle, will he show off pictures of himself in a Black and White striped shirt with Gazza on the back? I wouldn't be surprised any more."

A TEAM OF PLAYERS, I KNOW WOULD SWAP THE ROYAL BLUE SHIRT FOR A CLARET AND BLUE SHIRT IF IT MEANT EXTENDING THEIR CAREER OR EARNING THEM MORE MONEY!

Colin Withers
Stan Lynn
Curtis Davies
John Sleeuwenhoek
Liam Ridgewell
Craig Gardner
Geoff Vowden
Bruce Rioch
Des Bremner
Emile Heskey
Dwight Yorke
Substitutes: Malcolm Beard, Kevin Phillips, Peter Withe, Ron Wylie, Chris Sutton.

A TEAM OF PLAYERS, I BELIEVE WOULD NEVER SWAP THE ROYAL BLUE SHIRT FOR A CLARET AND BLUE SHIRT NO MATTER WHAT!
Gil Merrick
Ian Clarkson
Trevor Smith
Garry Pendrey
Malcolm Page
Darren Carter
Robbie Savage
Paul Tait
Kevan Broadhurst
Geoff Horsfield
Kenny Burns

Interesting?

- Billy George made 399 appearances in goal for Villa in the early 1900s. He joined Blues as a trainer but regular Blues goalkeeper Horace Bailey was injured and Billy stepped in at the last moment to make his one and only appearance in a blue shirt at the ripe old age of 37. Not surprisingly he is still the oldest player to make his debut for Blues.

- Joe Bradford never actually pulled on a claret and blue shirt as a professional but he did go there on trial as a teenager. They failed to see the potential which resulted in him becoming the Blues' top goalscorer with 249 goals in the sixteen seasons between 1920 and 1935.

- Des Bremner made nearly 200 appearances for Blues to go with his double-century of games for the Villa and was able to help Blues to promotion from the old Division Two in 1985.

- Doug Ellis crossed the divide via the Boardroom. He was a Director of Birmingham City in the 1960s before creating a consortium to take over Villa in 1969.

- Trevor Hockey played for Blues at his peak from 1965–1971 making 196 appearances and scoring eight goals. He made over 600 appearances for eight league clubs (including a season at Villa (1973–74) making 24 appearances and scoring a solitary goal. He played on all 92 football league grounds at the time. He released a record entitled "Happy Cos I'm Blue" which he performed at the Birmingham Town Hall.

5

THOUGHTS OF THE PLAYERS

I have been fortunate in my dealings with Birmingham City to meet a number of my heroes. Several of them have contributed to this book.

PAUL TAIT

Born in Sutton Coldfield on 31 July 1971, made 170 appearances for Blues scoring 14 goals.

I guess the first Blues player mentioned when talking about Blues and Villa rivalry is Paul Tait or "Taity". I will start off his contribution with an article I wrote for *"THE BLUES"* magazine in the series "My Time at The Blues". The article was never published as the magazine was closed down before it could be submitted, so after all this time, here it is:

"MY TIME AT THE BLUES" – PAUL RONALD TAIT

CAREER: 1987–1999
BLUES: YTS June 1987 Professional August 1988
MILLWALL: On Loan, February 1994
BOLTON WANDERERS: On Trial, July 1994
NORTHAMPTON TOWN: On Loan, December 1997
OXFORD: Free Transfer, January 1999 to May 2002
NEA SALAMIS (Cyprus)
HONOURS:
Blues: Division Two Champions, 1995
Auto-Windscreens Shield Winners, 1995
Appearances: 169 + 43 – 18 goals

"Can I help you with the door?" says a concerned Paul Tait as a lady struggles to get through a door at Starbucks in Solihull. "Thank You," replies the grate-

ful female as he tells me to get up and open the door! When you are in the company of "Taity" it's a real pleasure and there is always the unexpected. Relieved of my temporary doorman duties I ask him about his early years.

Paul Tait in that T-shirt

"My Dad is Scottish and my Mom's from Middlesbrough, they were living in Castle Vale when I came along, hence I was born at Good Hope Hospital in Sutton Coldfield. Two years later my sister Lauren was born and we were living in South Yardley. My Dad, Ronald is a Glasgow Rangers supporter and I saw my first game at Villa Park when I was about five. The game was billed as a friendly fixture but they didn't tell the Rangers' fans and they wrecked the place! I was watching from the safety of my Uncle's box in the Trinity Road stand and thought it must always be like this. It was riot and for me it's been like that ever since!"

Who signed you for Blues and how?

"When I was at Byng Kendrick School it was a rugby school, so it wasn't until my last year in the seniors that we managed to get one of the teachers to organise a football team. We did pretty well in our first and only season, winning a schools tournament. Matthew Fox who played for Blues was in the same team. After school I played for Hurley Colts, Near Atherstone and then Three C's who were based in Chelmsley Wood. It was whilst playing for them that Norman Bodell spotted me and Garry Pendrey signed me on YTS forms in June 1987 for a weekly age of £28.50. Blues were golden to me, when I was 12 I was playing with the Under 15s that included John Frain and Kevin Ashley. They would also take me on First Team trips they made a real fuss of me."

What do you remember of your debut?

"It was also my most memorable game, I was just 16 and it was against Leeds United at St Andrew's. It was played on a Friday night (6 May) to reduce the threat of any trouble. I was really scared when I came on after 28 minutes I must have done alright as I got Man of the Match, which shows how bad it was! But it was a great experience even though I froze in front of Mervyn Day their 'keeper and wasted a chance by hitting a post. It was the last match of the 1987–88 season and there was a crowd of 6,024. The team was: Hansbury; Frain, Roberts; Williams, Bird, Atkins; Handysides, Langley, Whitton, Russell, Wigley."

What was your most memorable goal?

"That was my first, scored against Walsall in September 1989 in a 2–0 victory. I picked the ball up from a corner at the Railway End and cut in from the left before bending it into the top left hand corner over Ron Green, which isn't that hard to do! I was originally a striker and it was "Crackers" Dave MacKay and Bobby Ferguson then asked me to take on the midfield role as I was the best runner in the club. I've always hated it in midfield because I couldn't tackle so I got lots of yellow cards!"

What was it like at Blues in those days?

"It was dire we used to train wherever we could find some space more often that not on the piece of parkland (well it's got swings) opposite the Garrison Pub. After Garry left, we had a number of stand-in managers, Steve Fleet and Bill Caldwell before Terry Cooper was appointed."

Tell me about your injury?

"It happened away against Leyton Orient on 12 January 1991. My knee was shattered and I was in tears, I was only 19. "Crackers" was always reluctant to send on the trainer you had to be virtually dead before he would sanction it. Anyway eventually the trainer came on and asked me, 'Can you walk?' a lot of good that was! I was referred to Professor David Dandy at Addenbroke's Hospital, Cambridge, he had sorted out Alan Shearer, but he took one look at my scan and predicted that I would never play at the top level again. I had to have a total knee reconstruction using bone from my hip but I did get back to playing some nine months later. It was scary when I came on as a sub in a friendly against Bristol City at Wast Hills. Once I'd survived that first tackle I was fine and went on to score.

"Whilst I was lucky to get fit again, the timing of the injury ruined my move to Spurs for £500k. I was being watched by Liverpool, Wolves and Spurs as an up and coming midfielder along with Jamie Redknapp. Liverpool went for him and my move to Spurs was imminent. Because it was a done deal I did not sign the contract renewal offered to me. As soon as I was injured seemingly never to play again Samesh Kumar got me to sign the contract so he could claim the insurance money. Bad Luck Samesh."

Why did you call Dave MacKay "crackers"?
"Cause he was crackers, he was a mad fan of Simon Sturridge, and all he ever said was, "Well Done Simon.""

Who were the characters during your time?
"The whole team had that Wimbledon "Crazy Gang" mentality we were like a prison team. Stand out characters were Mark Ward, Liam Daish and Gary Cooper, he was a real cockney wide boy."

How did you career end at Blues?
"Initially Baz (Barry Fry) tried to get me off the payroll with a loan spell at Millwall and a trial for Bolton. I spent six weeks at Millwall and never played a game as I was either ill or injured. They put me in a Bed and Breakfast in Eltham near their training ground and I got so bored I would drive back to Birmingham to see my mates and have a drink. On one occasion I missed training because of a late night/early morning and Mick McCarthy (their manager) called the loan spell off.

"Baz got me to go to Bolton supposedly to play in a pre-season game against Liverpool at Burnden Park, when I got there I was due to play the following day in the reserves against Millwall. I told them to forget it but it coincided with some bad press coverage on me so I guess they were pleased with my decision.

Paul Tait with Auto Windscreens Trophy

"Baz also nearly sold me to Watford for £250,000, the fee was agreed but before I went down I was told the deal was dead because someone from the West Midlands Police had told one of their Directors that I was trouble. So that put the kybosh on that deal.

"Eventually after nearly joining Dundee (I could never play against Rangers) I had a loan period with Ian Atkins at Northampton and played a couple of games, later I joined Oxford United on a free transfer in May 1999 and spent just over three years there. Then I went to play in Cyprus for five months. I stayed there for two years but stopped playing when they never paid me, eventually I did get paid in fivers, thank goodness my father-in-law who is a Cypriot acted as my interpreter. I knew things were going to be difficult when they showed me my club car. It was a very early Vauxhall Astra with flat tyres and no air conditioning!"

Note: If you ever get the chance to talk to Paul about his time at Oxford and an Irishman called Terry do so because the story is hilarious, as is his recollection of Malcolm Shotton's pre-match team talk!

What happened after that?

"Whilst coaching in the evenings I did a number of jobs, notably working for a maintenance company and for a year I was a postman in Redditch. After that the coaching got more and more and now I am full-time running Midlands Soccer Coaching which has centres in Redditch, Gloucester, Droitwich, Kidderminster and Banbury."

What do you think of the current Blues team?

"I don't think there is anyone in the team that would have given their team mates a real rollicking. In my day there was Daish, Dave Barnett and Kev Francis who would have really got it sorted in the dressing room."

How do you spend your time these days?

'I have not got time for hobbies although I'd like to play golf more, so I guess my real hobby is ensuring Rangers are always better than Celtic. Having said that my best mate is Devs (Paul Devlin) who was my room mate when we played together but he's a Celtic nut! I've also got four kids to keep me amused, Cameron Adam Luke and Sasha."

Why do you call TF "tricky"?

"At the start of every training session he would boot a ball as high as he could and then get it under control before it hit the ground, he had great skills."

How did you get on with Barry Fry?

"I loved him but if you were a true professional like John Frain it was murder. If training was called for 10 o'clock Frainy would be there dead on the dot and then Baz would roll up half an hour later."

Anything else?

"When Craig Brown was the Scotland International manager he wanted me to play for Scotland as my Dad was Scottish. I refused; why would I want to play for Scotland, I'm an Englishman. Tricky Francis was shocked that I'd turned down an International career.

"After we had got promoted from Division Three in 1992 there was a celebration party at The Cobden Hotel on the Hagley Road after the Shrewsbury game. I remember Samesh was dancing with Joan Hill (Commercial Manager) and I grabbed him in a headlock and proceeded to drag him around the dancefloor. What a night!

"Joan Hill was diamond to me as she would act as my taxi driver and get me home after a hectic post-match celebration."

Now what about that T-shirt?

"It was when I was getting off the coach for the Civic Reception with the Mayor that I found out the Football Association had charged me with bringing the game into disrepute and the club were going to fine me two weeks wages. It seemed like everyone was on my back apart from the real Bluenoses who understood the animosity against the Villa.

"Of course it was premeditated and after scoring the Golden Goal to win the Auto Windscreen Shield against Carlisle United it was the perfect opportunity to reveal my special T-shirt. It was only designed for my enjoyment and that of my team mates but of course it was seen live on Central and Border Television. What a rumpus? – Baz had to apologise to Aston Villa and hope that it would not affect our visit to play in Paul McGrath's testimonial. Politics. I was quoted as, 'It was a private joke, intended as a bit of a laugh. There was no malice intended. A lot of Aston Villa fans are friends of mine. If anybody takes it the wrong way, I'm perfectly willing to apologise'.

"Baz was quoted as saying, 'Paul's a talented footballer, but he's got to learn how to behave. I thought he had grown up a lot this season, and then he goes and does a daft thing like this'.

"David Sullivan was quoted as saying my action was 'very silly' even though he chastised me after the game for not talking to him about exploiting the commerciality of what I did but even the PFA had a go."

TERRY HENNESSEY

Born in Llay, Wales on 1 September 1942, made 178 appearances for Blues scoring three goals.

Terry remembers the occasion (1963 League Cup) not so much for the victory but the camaraderie that existed between the two sets of players in those days. "The victory was very sweet because it was always like World War III waiting to go off when we played them. But they were fantastic games and the one thing we had then, which you won't get now, was that off the field we were quite good mates. Don't get me wrong, we were hell bent on beating each other but players from both teams would usually meet up once a week for a few drinks. There was one player in their side we sussed out very quickly, though – a Scot called Charlie Aitken. Me being a silly Welshman, I always used to but the first round but by the time it used to come to his round, he'd had enough and used to go. I wouldn't say Charlie was tight but he'd wake up in the night to see if he'd lost any sleep. We got him back, though by winning the Cup!"

ROBERT HOPKINS

Made 173 appearances for Blue scoring 29 goals over two spells at St Andrew's.

Born in Small Heath on October 25 1961 Hoppy started out his professional career in 1979 at the city's other team Aston Villa and made a record-breaking debut by scoring with his first touch ten seconds after coming on as a substitute. He made his Blues debut in a 3-0 win with Notts County. "It was an immensely proud moment for me and for my dad who was watching in the stands."

Hoppy's full-blooded passion and 110 per cent effort endeared him to fans immediately – any player demonstrating these qualities is always taken to the hearts of the Bluenoses, "As long as you work hard the crowd will love you at Birmingham. So much so that they gave me my very own chant 'Singing I I Oppy Oppy I'.

"I have great memories of my first spell at Blues and playing with the team known as the "Crazy Gang" due to our battling performances. We were a team of battlers and yes I did have a bit of a bad boy reputation! But that was just the way we played, we had players like Mark Dennis and me who just got stuck in and worked hard."

Hoppy was transferred to Manchester City for a fee of £160,00 in September 1986 but later returned to the Midlands joining the Baggies in a £60,000 deal involving Imre Varadi who went to Maine Road in part-exchange. He enjoyed his time at The Hawthorns under Ron Saunders but when Brian Talbot replaced him Hoppy moved back to Blues on transfer deadline day March 1989 signing for Garry Pendrey.

"I let my heart rule my head really. I took a big pay cut to go back and then I found the club was in a real mess. The ground was in a state, the training ground had been sold so we had to train at St Andrew's or play five-a-side on the stadium car park if it was raining. It angered me really, the way things were being run and the penny-pinching. If there were four light bulbs in a room they would take out two. They even questioned how many sugars you had in your tea."

Robert Hopkins in Action

A slump to Division Three saw Pendrey and Dave Mackay go before Lou Macari was appointed. Hoppy suffered a final ignominy when, after sitting out Blues 1991 Leyland Daf Cup 3–2 victory over Tranmere Rovers at Wembley on the bench, he was told his services were no longer required via a telegram. "I would not have minded so much if they had told me to my face but to find out be telegram was pretty upsetting.

"Outside of the area I don't think people realise just quite how fierce the rivalry is. I know supporters in London, the North-East, Manchester, Liverpool will all say their derbies are big games, but the Birmingham derby is every bit as important. Those first couple of seasons in the Premier League we had a team of grafters, players who would put it in and get amongst and unsettle the opposition. You had Savage, Johnson, Horsfield, those types, and Villa didn't like it. The 3–0 and 2–0 double of 2002–03 will take some topping. For incident, performance, atmosphere – even Peter Enckelman's errors – those matches were quite something. Blues back in the top-flight after 16 years were the underdogs and relished the role as upstarts. I think we prefer it when it's like that. Right through the 70s, 80s and 90s we've been the underdogs and we've tended to raise ourselves for Villa. I think our supporters have been more up for it as well. It means more to us than to Villa. It probably doesn't help that most of their supporters don't come from Birmingham. I'd say the city is three-quarters Blues. I joined Villa from school as an apprentice in 1978 and made a handful of appearances before a swap deal was struck involving Alan Curbishley six years later. I was actually there for longer than I was at Blues. We won the FA Youth Cup and I was captain. But my heart was always at Blues. I think they knew that to be honest. I was rumbled one day at Notts County when I went to take a corner in front of the travelling contingent. I used to wear a Blues pin badge under my shirt. I stuck it underneath where the Villa crest was. Trouble was it popped out and all these Villa supporters saw it – they went mental. They wanted to clamber over and get at me. Funnily enough, it didn't make that big an issue at the time. Tony Barton, the manager, was under a lot of pressure then and you didn't get all the cameras at the grounds like you do now so I got away with it. When I played for Villa Reserves we used to kick off at 2pm. So after getting changed I would rush down to St Andrew's to see Blues in the second half. Whether it was out of loyalty to Blues the things I did, or stupidity, I don't know. When I joined Blues I was scared witless about how I would be received, to be honest. After my first game and when the word got out about me being a Blues supporter though they were – and still are – great to me. I played in about three or four derby games and I really enjoyed them. One sticks out in my mind was the one in the rain at Villa Park, when it was lashing it down. We lost 3–0 and Noel Blake missed a penalty and then got sent off after the whistle for dropping the nut on Steve McMahon. Afterwards there was a bit of a fracas in the Villa dressing room. They turned left after going down the tunnel, the away dressing room was on the right. A few of us got confused and took a wrong turn…accidentally on purpose. Let's just there was the sound of a few toilet doors slamming!

ROBBIE SAVAGE

Born in Wrexham, Wales on 18 October 1974, made 82 appearances for Blues scoring 11 goals.

In his autobiography "*SAVAGE*" he recalls:

"Aston Villa. The team I loved to beat. The first Second City derby for years was always going to be a hell of an occasion. This was a match between the princes and the paupers. Villa were the all-stars and we were working-class grafters. I wasn't really aware of the hatred between the two sets of supporters until I joined Birmingham. All I can say is thank you to Olof Mellberg. I really didn't like him, but he did us a massive favour in the run-up to the game by saying he hadn't heard of any of us because we'd just been promoted. Er, Olof, I'm the guy who made Villa's life a misery at Leicester – and played the last five years in the Premier League. Brucie told us to remember those words, and we did. Mellberg was hopeless that night too. I'd been a real jinx to Villa during my years at Leicester, but that was a different situation. It was a battle. That was the only way to describe it. I still don't know what the police were doing playing it at night. St Andrew's was electric. Bluenoses were going mad, and the Villa fans were making a noise too. It has to go down as one of the best atmospheres I have ever played in. And we won 3–0

"The first goal was going to be crucial. Aliou Cisse and I bossed the game, and Clinton (Morrison) scored the opener. I looked around me, and there were fights breaking out everywhere. The second goal will go down in the history books (Author's note: You were right there – here it is) as one of the most bizarre goals ever. Mellberg took a throw-in, and the ball rolled under Peter Enckelman's foot and straight into the net. I still don't know whether Enckelman touched it or not, but his reactions suggested that he had done. The goal was given anyway. Then a fan ran onto the pitch and slapped Pete across the face.

"The tackles were flying in, and they had a goal disallowed by David Elleray, much to the disgust of Graham Taylor. Hors (Geoff Horsfield) made sure near the end when he robbed Alpay. The Bluenoses were singing 'We love you Robbie, because you've got blond hair'. I won't tell you what the Villa fans were singing!

"I was Sky's Man of the Match. It was an incredible night, and it gives me goose-pimples just to think about it again. I was still undefeated against Villa, and the Birmingham supporters fell in love with me. I epitomised what they wanted. I may not have had the best technical ability in the world, but I would give it a go. I was honest and hard-working, and they could relate to that. When they went to work, they could imagine they were like me: a trier and a fighter. Cheers Olof.

"Villa again. Three points guaranteed. Unbelievably, given the scenes in the first derby, this was another night kick-off. Both sets of fans behaved diabolically too. It was so emotionally charged. We went there buoyant from the win over Liverpool. Skippy headed in Jeff Kenna's cross at the back post, and Hors made sure. That doesn't begin to tell the story though. Dublin was sent off for head-butting me, Joey Gudjonson went for a two-footed tackle on Upson, and a couple of fans ran onto the pitch – and one approached me. Peter Enckelman in the Villa goal couldn't handle it. The second goal was the 'keeper's ball, but Peter hesitated and Hors tapped it into an empty net. People went mad up in the sponsors' box. I was wondering whether I'd get out of there alive. Mark Halsey was the ref that night, and I bet he's never forgotten it.

"I'm not quite sure why Dion has it in for me. I played up front with him at Manchester United and we were fine then. It is widely known now that he doesn't like me at all. Maybe he holds a grudge because I am more popular than him in his own town of Leicester. We've had similar careers: broken necks, broken legs. He was a decent player, though not a world-beater, and the same could be said of me. I respected what he did. I'm very pleased I saw the tackle coming that day. It was a red-card offence by itself. "Fucking Wanker!" I yelled at him. He walked over and butted me. "Prick" was his response.

"Look at the footage. I didn't do anything wrong. Dublin's tackle was appalling, and he butted me. Not the other way round. Dublin had a bad disciplinary record. He was sent off quite a few times. Everybody has a dirty tackle in them. What really annoyed me was that afterwards everyone presumed Dublin had lost it because I'd made a racist comment. He wouldn't have done it otherwise, would he? I am grateful that Dublin came out straight away to knock that one on the head, but it saddens me that he holds a grudge. If he met me and still thought I was a wanker, fair enough.

"Brucie did the right thing and took me off. Coins, lighters, everything was being thrown at me. I thought I was going to be hit and knocked out. We were in the dressing room for an hour, and we couldn't get out. It was incredible. I was glad I'd told my family to stay away. Heard of us now, Mellberg? We climbed onto the team coach, and the fans were throwing coins at the bus and hurling insults. My middle finger was up to the fans.

"Don't do anything stupid, had been Brucie's instruction as we left the changing-room. And we were giving them the finger! We drove back to the training ground, and dozens of fans were waiting for us. They were shouting and cheering because we'd done something amazing: we'd done the double over Aston Villa. Villa were the bigger club historically, but we'd beaten them twice. Unbelievable. Villa lost the plot that night. In Birmingham, 50 per cent of the fans love you and want to buy you a drink, and 50 per cent hate you and want to kill you. The city centre was a no-go area for weeks after the game. It was one of those fixtures where you thought someone could get killed. I received death threats afterwards."

KEVAN BROADHURST

Born in Dewsbury on 3 June 1959, made 153 appearances for Blues scoring 10 goals.

Kevan Broadhurst reckons that punch-ups will ALWAYS be part of a Second City derby. The former Blues centre-half, now assistant manager at Bristol Rovers, watched last week's post-match flare-up on the pitch between Lee Hendrie and Mario Melchiot with a wry smile.

Broadhurst was involved in some heated local derbies in his time, including the 1983 game at Villa Park that was christened the Demolition Derby. In that fiery clash Broadhurst was the victim of a career-threatening tackle by Steve McMahon, while Colin Gibson was sent off for Villa.

Robert Hopkins and Dennis Mortimer were involved in a running feud all game and Noel Blake took his own form of retribution on McMahon with a head-butt after the final whistle.

Villa won thanks to a Peter Withe goal – but just like last week – there was also a scuffle in the tunnel afterwards for good measure.

Unproved reports have suggested that there may well have been some "afters" in the tunnel following Blues' 2–0 win last week, but Broadhurst believes it shows that players care in what is one of the most highly-charged derbies in the country. The hatred between the two sets of supporters has been well documented, and it has spilt over onto the pitch all too frequently.

Yet Broadhurst reckons you will never take away the edge that exists between the two sets of players. "The game means so much to the city that if you lose it lasts a hell of a long time." He said, "It's not as though you can play them again next week and you have to suffer for around six months to try and make amends. After-match fights are nothing new. We had one in 1983. I had been stretchered off but by all accounts there was a fracas in the tunnel afterwards and I think ITV cameras picked it up. Noel Blake and Steve McMahon had their own little tussle as well, but I don't think it is a problem as it shows people care. I still work in the game and I sometimes question how much defeat hurts players nowadays. It would have been a case of exchanging views in the tunnel and then 30 minutes later you were buying that same person a drink in the bar. It is all forgotten and that is the way it should be. It is just a storm in a teacup. I have been involved in pre-match tunnel fights as well. It is all part of the psychological battle that goes on in football."

The players involved in the derby 22 years ago are vastly different from the 2005 version. Then it was an all-British affair with a large percentage of players from Birmingham itself. Of the teams that started last week, however, only Darren Carter, Stefan Moore and Lee Hendrie were born in the Second City.

Yet Broadhurst, who originates from Yorkshire, reckons it does not take long to get caught up in the frenzied rivalry. "The managers would certainly be winding the players up during the build-up to the game and stressing how important it is to the club and fans." Added Broadhurst.

"Birmingham is a very cosmopolitan city now but you still live and mix with all the locals and become a part of the infrastructure. You are constantly surrounded by fans of both clubs and they don't like it if they have been beaten. I can't see it changing whoever plays in these games because it means so much to the fans and they won't let it. I played against Albion, Wolves and Coventry and none of them run this game close for rivalry."

Broadhurst also reckoned that Blues deserved to pick up all three points in last weeks red-hot derby showdown. But he believes that Blues' fourth win in the last six derbies rubbed Villa's nose in it enough and that the late showboating wasn't necessary. "Blues were the better team and deserved to win," he continued, "If I were a Villa player, though I think I would have been wound up at the end by Blues playing keep-ball. I could handle getting beaten when I played but if I thought someone was taking the mickey then I would be annoyed. It was a little bit unnecessary. I can remember that when you won a derby game it was very satisfying and your supporters felt quite arrogant and cocky until the next game. If you lost then you felt a little bit downtrodden. A draw is the best result all round because it keeps everyone happy and there are generally no problems after the game either."

Author's note: Trouble began to brew on the field when Villa's Lee Hendrie took exception to Blues' Mario Melchiot "showboating" in stoppage-time of Blues' 2–0 win. Melchiot, according to Blues sources, had apparently been angered by Hendrie earlier in the game when his hand was stamped on after a tackle. As tempers began to fray in the tunnel and players traded insults, Hendrie took exception to a threat and 'it all went off', an eyewitness who did not want to be named, told the *Evening Mail*. "Blues striker Emile Heskey and Villa goalkeeper Stefan Postma are believed to have clashed before club officials, stewards and security guards managed to restore order". *Evening Mail* Colin Tattum 24/03/2005

KEN LEEK

Born in Ynysybwl, Wales on 26 July 1935, made 104 appearances for Blues scoring 49 goals. He died on 19 November 2007 at the age of 72.

I had the great pleasure to meet Ken at his home in Northampton when I was invited there to interview him for *THE BLUES* magazine.

"I've still got my 1963 League Cup Winners tankard displayed in the cabinet at home. It's there with the mementoes that I picked up whilst playing for Wales. I like to show them to my grandchildren to show them that their granddad wasn't a bad player. I scored two goals in the final against Aston Villa but I don't really remember much about them, I do remember that the games were quite a big occasions, even though the Final wasn't played at Wembley in those days. With it being a local derby you had to put in that little bit extra for the sake of the fans. We had some good lads at the club in those days and the team spirit was terrific. Our style of play suited me down to the ground. As a striker you rely upon the service from your colleagues and with Mike Hellawell and Bertie Auld on the wings and Terry Hennessey prompting from wing-half, I was always likely to get a few chances in a game. I think that my days with the Blues were the happiest part of my playing career."

Although Ken rejoices in that success over the Villa he has to have a soft spot for the Claret and Blues as his grandson Karl Darlow spent over eight years in their Academy before becoming a professional footballer like his granddad.

Author's Note: Ken's grandson was born on 8 October 1990 and is currently playing for Nottingham Forest as a goalkeeper. He was released by the Villa at the age of 16 and on the recommendation of Eric Steele (the Villa's goalkeeping coach at the time) he joined the Forest Academy progressing through the reserves to his first-team debut as a substitute against Crystal Palace on the final day of the 2010–11 season. After loan period at Newport County and Walsall he secured a contract at Forest through to 2015. He first full league debut happened on 12 January 2013 against Peterborough. Although eligible to play for Wales due to Ken being born in Ynysybwl he declined an invitation to join the Welsh squad for a friendly in February 2013.

IAN CLARKSON

Born in Solihull on 4 December 1970, made 136 appearances for Blues without scoring a goal.

"As a five-year-old I stood on the St Andrew's terraces in 1976 and watched Howard Kendall, my hero, score a goal in the old first division, dreaming of one day gracing the hallowed turf myself. I achieved my dream and went on to make 172 appearances for the Blues between 1988 and 1993. It is every Blue-nose's dream to line up against Aston Villa at St Andrew's. Few enjoy the opportunity to live out their fantasies but my wish came true on September 27 1988, when as a callow 17-year-old I stepped on to my field of dreams to face our ancient rivals in a League Cup second round, first-leg tie.

"Sadly the night ended in a 2–0 defeat at the hands of our neighbours from across the city but 25 years on I still look back on that autumn evening with immense pride.

"We lost, but if someone had told me I'd make my debut for Blues, against the Villa, I could probably have died next day a fairly happy man. It came from nowhere really and I hadn't been in the squad, but we'd had a ropey start in the old second division and were near the bottom. Garry Pendrey, the manager, didn't have much cash to buy new players, but we had quite a good youth side in those days and, after training in the morning, he put me in the squad for the Villa game. I turned up at St Andrew's not expecting to see my name in the line-up, but Vince Overson gave me a massive slap on the back and said, 'All the best, son' and there I was at number six.

"I was nervous , couldn't sit down, so Tony Godden took me out for a bit of a warm up. It was a nerve-racking experience and David Platt and Gary Thompson were playing for Villa, but even though we lost I enjoyed the game.

"Yes I did, it was Second Round League Cup first leg on 27 September 1988 at St Andrew's, we lost 0–2 in front of 21,177. The team that day was:

TONY GODDEN, RAY RANSON, HARRY ROBERTS, IAN ATKINS, VINCE OVERSON, IAN CLARKSON, RONNIE MORRIS, KEVIN LANGLEY, MARK YATES, COLIN ROBINSON, STEVE WIGLEY
– sub: DES BREMNER. We lost the second leg 5-0!

BOBBY THOMSON

Born in Dundee on 21 March 1937, made 114 appearances for Blues scoring 23 goals.

Stan Cullis was convinced that Bobby was a wing-half but Joe Mercer, Manager of Aston Villa had different ideas and signed Bobby in June 1959 as a goalscoring forward, Bobby re-paid Joe with 70 goals in 171 appearances resulting in promotion from Division Two and a League Cup triumph.

Not long after Blues beat Villa in 1963 League Cup Final, Trevor Smith opened the door to the communal bathroom and announced to his teammates the signing of Bobby, the universal response was "Things can't be that bad".

Bobby never had any problem with the Bluenoses regarding his time with Villa and recalls how he was never booed by the St Andrew's crowd as they always seemed to respect the fact that in every game he gave his all.

In the five seasons he was at Blues, he scored 26 goals in 129 appearances and wore the following shirts, numbers 4, 6, 8, 9, 10 and 12.

It was as a substitute that Bobby featured in a 5–5 draw with Derby County at St Andrew's. "I had had quite a late night and was relieved to be given the number 12 shirt after Denis Thwaites had been passed fit, sitting in the dug-out I had the sun in my bleary eyes throughout the game and when I had to replace the injured Ronnie Fenton I could barely see; due to the sun, I swear.

"The thing that strikes me about these derby games now is how the rivalry can get out of hand. The Blues fans shout 'Something on the Villa' and the Villa fans shout 'Something on the Blues' and that puts me bang off. In my days the players used to socialise together and the fans did too and there was a lot more respect for each other – I'd like to see that return"

Just months after the League Cup Final games Thomson proved the closeness between the clubs by becoming one of a handful of players to cross the Second City divide. In September 1963 he travelled the 3.6 miles from Villa Park to St Andrew's to swap Villa for Blues – and all for an extra 25 quid a week. Writing in his autobiography *"The Real Bobby Dazzler"* he reveals: "I went in to see Joe Mercer in his office. He was there with his feet up on the table. 'I'm going to sign for Blues boss. I only want a tenner extra' Joe didn't want me to leave, but the club financiers wouldn't budge and refused to pay me extra. I was off to Blues for an extra £25 or £35 per week. I had given my heart to Villa over the previous four years, player in five different positions and scored 70 goals. I was sad to leave but it was time to move on."

BERTIE AULD

Born in Glasgow on 23 March 1938, made 126 appearances for Blues scoring 26 goals.

"I was extremely proud to be part of that Birmingham team winning the trophy. And I'll tell you this; it was just as big a thrill as winning the European Cup after I went back to Celtic. At the time, the European Cup was looked at a lot differently. It was only with the passing of the years what we all understood what an achievement it was and how it became more and more important to us and everyone else. We were the first British side to win it, but those two games against Villa meant just as much. It was satisfying. I was part of a great group of players and great characters, people who took a great pride in themselves and how they played. The final, being a derby games was very important to us. I vividly remember making that walk out of the long tunnel under the stand from the dressing room at St Andrew's to the centre of the park and being hit by this incredible sound, like you were in a music studio – it was hitting you from everywhere. It was inspiring and we felt we could win, and we played well. What also stuck with me was what Gil said just before we went our. Gil was always on about having respect for everybody, and that was his team talk. He spoke about them as individuals and as a team and said we should have respect for them, but that he felt we had a better team and we all knew what we could achieve if we played together. He told us to try and entertain and enjoy it 'because you are no sooner playing until you are watching', meaning before we knew it our careers would be over so we had to make the most of an opportunity like a final."

IAN ATKINS

Born in Sheldon on 16 January 1957, made 101 appearances for Blues scoring six goals during two spells at St Andrew's.

"It was the second leg of the League Cup Second Round in 1988–89 season and we were already 2–0 down from the first leg at St Andrew's. We had actually played very well in the game but Villa were very strong then, they had some big players and the momentum of the club was going again. Graham Taylor set up his teams to put you under pressure; they always went for the forward ball. And there was no way he was not going to be playing anything other than his strongest side in the second leg. We knew what was coming, but it was too much. They steamrollered us; the tempo and players they has was just too much. Back then at Blues it was scary. You tended to know the end result of games before you had even started, as the club was in such a mess. They were awful days. Garry Pendrey had to pick half a dozen teenagers because of injuries and a thin squad and matters were not helped by Tony Godden being ruled out, then another older campaigner coming off in the game. It was as if the white flag was being raised by Blues. After their third goal I looked round and wondered 'where's Ray Ranson?' and there he was hobbling off. You can't publish the words I shouted to him but I wasn't very complimentary. It was galling, as a local lad, coming back to Blues and what we went through in those days. I signed from Ipswich Town and I was told it was going to be this, going to be that. The training ground at Elmdon was going to be the best in the Midlands, but it had not changed since I was at Sheldon Heath Comprehensive. We had one light bulb and an electric fire. I remember once I put on the second bar and it fused all the electrics in the place. That summed Blues up then. The club was decaying and the better players that we did have – Steve Wigley, Steve Whitton – ended up leaving. The only good thing about that season in which we were relegated to Division Three for the first time in our history was that we had the young lads like John Frain, Ian Clarkson, Paul Tait, Dean Peer, Mark Yates and Simon Sturridge coming through. By the end of the season there was Martin Thomas, Harry Roberts and me and that was it of the experienced ones."

WINSTON FOSTER

Born in Birmingham on 1 November 1941, made 152 appearances for Blues scoring two goals.

"There has been rivalry between Villa, and all the local clubs in the area where you live; be it, Albion or Wolves, but Villa has always been the most intense, especially for supporters who have to work along side supporters from these clubs. I used to live in the same road as Harry Burrows of Villa, and we had leisure time in each others house with our wives, but when on the pitch as opponents, we were the best of enemies. The following week we would be in one or the others house having a glass of wine with our wives again, but on the pitch we would be kicking lumps out of each other, because at the end of the day we were both professional footballers doing our job!!"

MARTIN THOMAS

Born in Senghenydd, Wales on 28 November 1959, made 144 appearances for Blues.

Although I went to Villa for a month on cover…I only ended up playing one reserve game v Man Utd (at Bescot) before returning to Blues after a fortnight as the GKs were all then fit.

The Training facilities at Bodymoor Heath were terrific, Blues had moved into their current complex at Wast Hills and had started to develop it…one thing they both had in common was the wind!!! On a bad day you could not put a cone down without it blowing the length of the training area.

Good to see that Blues have now further developed their base, with the Villa first team now moving to an extended complex on the same "Bodymoor" site.

6

"CROSSING THE DIVIDE – ALEX MCLEISH AND RON SAUNDERS"

There have been two managers who crossed the line and both provoked intense negative reaction from the Blues fans; Ron Saunders was recruited behind the scenes resulting in the popular Jim Smith being removed from his job behind his back and Alex McLeish who having taken Blues to Wembley glory and relegation to The Championship sought to maintain his earnings by moving to the hot seat in Witton, causing delight amongst the Bluenoses and derision from the Villa fans.

There is little doubt that McLeish's departure caused the greatest uproar due in part to the increased media options in the 21st century than back in 1982 when Saunders defected.

It is my belief that neither man expected the negative reaction their appointments would provoke from both sets of fans, as a Scouser and a Glaswegian would underestimate the bad blood which exists between the two Birmingham-based clubs.

In football terms both managers have good testimonials:

	RON SAUNDERS	ALEX McLEISH
Date of Birth	6 November 1932	20 January 1959
Place of Birth	Birkenhead, England	Glasgow, Scotland
Position as Player	Striker	Central-Defender
Playing Career	Everton 1951–55 3 apps. 0 goals	Aberdeen 1978–94 493 apps 25 goals
	Tonbridge Angels 1955–57	Motherwell 1994–95 3 apps 0 goals
	Gillingham 1957–58 49 apps 20 goals	Scotland U-21 197887 6 apps 0 goals
	Portsmouth 236 apps 145 goals	Scotland 1980–1993 77 apps 0 goals

	Watford 39 apps 18 goals	
	Charlton Athletic 65 apps 24 goals	
Managerial Career	Yeovil Town 1967–69	Motherwell 1994–98
	Oxford United 1969	Hibernian 1998–2001
	Norwich City 1969–73	Glasgow Rangers 2001–06
	Manchester City 1973–74	Scotland 2007
	Aston Villa 1974–82	Blues 2007–2011
	Blues 1982–86	Aston Villa 2011–2012
	West Bromwich Albion 1986–87	Nottingham Forest 2012–2013
Honours as Manager	Norwich City Promotion 1972	Motherwell Scottish Premier Runners-Up 1994–95
	Aston Villa League Cup Winners 1975 and 1977 and Promotion 1975	Hibernian Scottish First Division 1998–99 Scottish Cup Runners-Up 2000–01
	Aston Villa First Division Champions 1980–81	Rangers Scottish Premier 2002–03 and 2004–05 Scottish Cup 2001–02 and 2002–03 Scottish League Cup 2002, 2003 and 2005
	Blues Promotion to Division One 1984-85	Blues Championship Runners-Up 2008–09 League Cup 2010–11
Honours as Player		Scottish Premier 1979–80, 1983–84 and 1984–85 Scottish Cup 1981–82, 1982–83, 1983–84, 1985–86 and 1989–90 Scottish League Cup 1985–86 and 1989–90 European Cup Winners Cup 1982–83 European Super Cup 1983 1980-81 Division One Champions

ALEX MCLEISH

Mcleish will always be remembered for the Carling Cup win against Arsenal at Wembley and to a certain extent that eased the level of hate which he engendered by moving to Villa Park. His first return to St Andrew's was during his short time managing Nottingham Forest and although he received considerable verbal abuse it was never at the level the press expected (hoped for) as the Bluenoses respected what he had achieved at Wembley.

The Villa fans did not want him for two reasons – his time at St Andrew's and his style of football which was probably best described by Alexander Hleb who after his loan period with the Blues from Barcelona described Big Eck's training as "Kicking the ball as high and as hard as possible and chase after it as hard as you can!" or as reported in the *Birmingham Mail*:

Alexander Hleb who played 19 times for Birmingham City under Alex McLeish has criticised the tactics of his former manager. "At Birmingham, the day before a game he would come onto the pitch and show us what to do: You stand here, the goalkeeper will give you the ball here, kick it as far as you can and don't pass to anyone nearby. And we all run."

He was a central defender for Aberdeen in the 1980s making nearly 500 appearances for the club winning 77 caps for Scotland. His managerial career began with time at Motherwell and Hibernian before leading Glasgow Rangers to two championships and five cup wins in five years. He spent ten months as manager of the Scottish national team, which very nearly qualified for the 2008 UEFA European Championships. He left in November 2007 to join Blues who were in the Premier League only to get relegated at the end of his first season. He led them back in 2009 to go on to win the Football League Cup in 2011 beating Arsenal but also being relegated at the end of that successful season. Following relegation he deserted St Andrew's to become manager of Aston Villa making him the first manager to move directly from Blues to Villa and only the second manager after Ron Saunders to manage both clubs. Villa narrowly avoided relegation in 2011–12 his contract was terminated by Villa at the end of his first season. He was later appointed as manager of Championship Club Nottingham Forest in December 2012 leaving 40 days later after being beaten by Blues at St Andrew's.

His service to Scottish sport won him an honorary doctorate at Aberdeen University in 2008.

He was born in Duke Street Hospital Glasgow to parents Alex, a shipyard worker and Jean. He has a younger brother Ian and a younger sister Angela. After living in the Parkhead and Kinning Park districts of Glasgow the family moved to Barrhead, Renfrewshire when he was around five years of age. He attended Springhill Primary, Barrhead High School and John Neilson High School in Paisley.

As a young footballer he played for Barrhead Youth Club, alongside Weir and Glasgow United as well as training for a short period with Hamilton Academicals. He was signed for Aberdeen by Ally MacLeod in 1976 after a local Cup Final in Glasgow.

After two seasons in the reserve side and a loan period at Lewis United he made his debut against Dundee United on 2 January 1978. His first major final appearance was as a substitute in a 2–1 defeat to Glasgow Rangers in the 1978–79 Scottish League Cup the manager at the time was Alex Ferguson. In the ensuing seven seasons he won eight domestic and two European trophies. He scored a rare goal in the 4–1 win over Glasgow Rangers in the 1982 Scottish Cup Final which coincided with his 200th appearance for the Dons. He was Scottish player of the year in 1990 eventually captaining the side after Willie Miller's retirement.

He is Scotland's third most capped player having made 77 international appearances between 1980 and 1993. He played in three World Cups in 1982, 1986 and 1990. He captained the national side against Luxembourg in 1987 which coincided with him winning his 50th cap. His final international game was on 17 February 1993 in a 3–0 win over Malta at Hampden Park during the 1994 World Cup qualifiers. He is a member of the Scottish Football Hall of Fame and the Scotland National Football Team Roll of Honour.

He was appointed manager of Motherwell in 1994 twelve months after retiring as a player, he joined Hibernian in 1998 guiding them back into the Scottish Premier Division in 1999 after their relegation in 1998 – do we see a familiar pattern developing?

After being awarded his UEFA Pro Licence he joined Glasgow Rangers in December 2001. He won the Scottish Cup and Scottish League Cup in his first season, achieving the domestic treble the year after by winning the League title. He won the 2005 League title taking Rangers into the knockout stages of the Champions League for the first time getting to the last 16 before being beaten by Villarreal on the away goals rule. He became Scotland's manager on 29 January 2007.

He moved to Blues on 28 November 2007 after attending the draw for 2010 FIFA World Cup in South Africa taking his Scottish assistants Roy Aitken and Andy Watson to St Andrew's.

His first game with Blues ended in a 3–2 away win to Tottenham Hotspur.

On the final day of the 2008–09 season, McLeish secured Birmingham's return to the top flight of English football at the first attempt with a 2–1 away victory over Reading. By mid-January 2010, he had guided them to a 12-game unbeaten run, a club record in the top division, set a Premier League record by selecting the same starting eleven for nine consecutive games, and been named Premier League Manager of the Month for December 2009, the first Birmingham manager to receive the award. By the end of the season McLeish had led Birmingham to ninth place, their highest finish for more than 50 years.

Following Birmingham›s success during the 2009–10 season, McLeish agreed a new three-year deal with the club in September 2010. In February 2011, McLeish led Birmingham to victory in the League Cup, defeating favourites Arsenal 2–1 in the final at Wembley in what he described as "relatively speaking… [his] greatest achievement." However, a poor run of form followed the League Cup win, and Birmingham were relegated to the Championship on the last day of the 2010–11 season. The directors confirmed that McLeish would keep his job, and would be expected to return the club to the Premier League at the first opportunity. McLeish however opted to quit Birmingham City on 12 June 2011 by email.

On 23 May 2011 all Bluenoses who subscribe to receiving e-mail updates from the club received the following e-mail from "Big Eck".

Dear Keith

It was a rollercoaster afternoon for us all yesterday, and of course I am disappointed and upset, just as everyone else connected with the club is.

But I'm not going to talk at length about my feelings. That would be selfish because we are a club and everyone connected with Birmingham City will be feeling this, not least the supporters who were absolutely magnificent as always.

There was a deadly silence after the game in the dressing room, the players were hurting and that's because they care.

I will not make excuses for finishing third bottom of the Barclays Premier League but I believe there were certain factors that contributed to things. Every team has injuries, of course they do, but I think it's fair to say our treatment room was busier than most, particularly since the Carling Cup Final.

We didn't score enough goals as a team – there is no individual blame to be handed out there, because goals are scored as a unit – and at a time when the likes of Zigic and Martins were starting to hit the back of the net they were cut down in their prime.

That was the case with several other of our players – I don't need to list them all because thay have been well documented – and that didn't help our cause.

We have to pay tribute to the Barclays Premier League because the exceptionally high quality this season means that teams are going down with 39 points, which would be more than enough to keep them up most of the time.

Everyone is hurting right now and we all need time to reflect on what has happened before making sure we bounce back, because it's important that we do that.

Your support at White Hart Lane yesterday was phenomenal and that was appreciated by all. Even after the final whistle you kept on singing and I salute you for that unwavering support.

WITHIN TWENTY DAYS HE WAS GONE!

McLeish received death threats from followers of both teams following his appointment as Aston Villa manager. This controversial move only increased tension and hostility between the players, supporters and owners of both clubs even more as Blues directors threatened legal action against Villa for allegedly "tapping up" McLeish, who resigned as Blues manager on 12 June 2011, while he was still under contract at Birmingham City.

On 17 June 2011, Aston Villa appointed McLeish as manager, just five days after leaving their local rivals Birmingham City.

There was much controversy surrounding his appointment as Birmingham City claimed McLeish was still under contract and filed a complaint against Aston Villa to the Premier League while Villa claimed McLeish was a free agent.

Aston Villa fans protested outside Villa Park and anti-McLeish graffiti had to be removed from outside Villa's training ground. McLeish led the 2011–12 Villa team to 16th place in the Premier League, avoiding relegation by two points, and set an unwanted club record of only four home wins. McLeish's contract was terminated on 14 May, the day after the season ended. The reasons cited for his termination were the poor results and style of play used throughout his term as manager. McLeish currently holds the record for being statistically the worst manager of Aston Villa, with a win percentage of only 21 per cent. His win percentage at Blues was 36.9 per cent - Played 168 won 62 drew 51 lost 55 (Overall Played 782 won 359 drew 201 lost 222 win percentage 45.91).

McLeish was appointed manager of Nottingham Forest on 27 December 2012 after a 2–1 defeat to former club Birmingham City on his first return to St Andrew's, he refused to commit his future to Nottingham Forest and claimed he was unhappy. On 5 February 2013, he left the club by mutual consent.

The only good thing about the betrayal by McLeish on the Blues was the fact that it seriously angered the Villa fans. Whilst Bluenoses were angry at "Big Eck" for the betrayal the Villa fans were out at Villa Park and Bodymoor Heath protesting that not only was he ex-Blues but he had been in charge whilst Blues were relegated twice from the Premier League. His style of football did not endear him to the Villa faithful. His appointment was seen to be lacking in ambition and also negative!

It could not happen to a better club!

The following report appeared in *The Daily Mirror*:
"Birmingham's Second City rivalry with Aston Villa is set to reach dangerous new levels of tension after Alex McLeish's shock resignation. City's directors

are fuming after manager McLeish quit with a business-like email yesterday – just three weeks after the club stood by him as the club were relegated. And Blues fans are also raging after learning the Scot is now odds-on favourite with bookies to take charge at nearby managerless Villa.

"And even rival Villa supporters are unimpressed at the prospect of taking the boss of their relegated neighbours.

"But it is City's hierarchy – who have received no approach from Villa – who are especially livid after publicly backing McLeish following relegation from the Premier League.

"St Andrew's owner Carson Yeung stood by McLeish this summer as scout Paul Montgomery was the fall guy. Brum have since signed three Bosmans – Marlon King, Chris Burke and Senegalese midfielder Morgaro Gomis from Dundee United at McLeish's request. The club's acting chairman Peter Pannu was also in Amsterdam yesterday negotiating for PSV Eindhoven's Danny Koevermans when McLeish suddenly quit. And Pannu contacted *Mirrorsport* to explain City's board feel betrayed by McLeish and are planning legal action.

"Pannu, a former Hong Kong cop and barrister, said: "We have just brought in three players of his choice, and whilst in Amsterdam, having secured him the fourth one, an email on Sunday when I am on business speaks volumes. We spent £40million, supported him all the way and what we get is a relegation and a snub when Carson gave him unwavering support and did not sack him.

"We declared his job secure and professed trust and confidence in him, so much so we have just negotiated four of his new first choice players. I won't blame any outside clubs yet until I find out more.

"He is still our contracted staff and BCFC does not grant him any right to speak to any outsiders until the matter is resolved. I will be meeting my legal team on Monday. I will deal with this and rest assured I will leave no stones unturned. It's about time some discipline is instilled into this game and I am unfortunately not a person who gets pushed about."

The following report appeared in the local press:
Alex McLeish insists he will prove the right man for Aston Villa after signing a three-year deal as their controversial choice of boss.

Villa is close to agreeing a compensation deal with Birmingham – believed to be in the region of £2million – although the Blues insist they remain in a legal fight. McLeish has now vowed to show why Villa owner Randy Lerner was right to take a gamble on him.

First steps:
Alex McLeish arrives at Villa Park after being confirmed as the club's new manager.

After being confirmed at 9am this morning, he said: "I am honoured to have this opportunity to manage a club with such a fantastic history as Aston Villa's. The heritage, the history of success and the tradition of Aston Villa are compelling and irresistible. The challenge for me is to try to add my own chapter. Since first becoming a manager at Motherwell, my desire to succeed and my energy and drive have never waned. My objective is to impart that drive and will to win to the players and fans of Aston Villa. I know that some of our fans have voiced concerns and I can understand why. It will be up to me to convince you that I am the right man to drive the club forward and I intend to give absolutely everything to prove that I can be a success at the club."

The 52-year-old became Villa manager six days after resigning from their city rivals with two years left on his contract. He will succeed Gerard Houllier, who left the job after less than a year because of health problems.

Uproar:
Aston Villa supporters protest against McLeish on the steps outside Villa Park on Wednesday

McLeish spent most of Wednesday locked in talks with Villa owner Randy Lerner, only for lawyers to become involved after Birmingham threatened an injunction to stop their former manager taking the job.

Villa chief executive Paul Faulkner said: "We believe we have appointed the right man for the job.

Unquestionably, Alex meets the criteria we set out at the beginning of our search which was based on proven Premier League experience, leadership, a hard-working ethic and, most importantly, a shared vision for Aston Villa.

"Alex is someone with whom we will work close and work well together. With our strong squad combining the necessary virtues of experience and the exciting potential of our young players, our objective is to compete as strongly as we possibly can.

"Alex's vast experience and proven abilities demonstrate clearly that he is a strong leader and an ambitious man and we are looking forward very much to the exciting new season about to start."

Birmingham has insisted they will continue their legal fight over McLeish's exit.

A club statement read: "The fact that Alex McLeish has been appointed as manager of Aston Villa does not, in any way, mean that the legal dispute is over and Birmingham City Football Club maintains its stance and shall vigorously pursue the matter.

"We are very disappointed with how the club and its fans have been treated by Mr McLeish given the way we have supported him over the years and we are still looking into whether Aston Villa's conduct has been in line with Premier League rules.

"As the club is currently enforcing its legal right with Mr McLeish the matter is in the hands of our lawyers and it is therefore not appropriate for the club to make any further comment at this stage.

"The club will continue its full efforts on recruiting a new manager and hope to make an appointment as soon as possible."

McLeish has also been given an immediate seal of approval from the Premier League's Godfather.

Sir Alex Ferguson is delighted with the appointment. McLeish's mentor and friend believes that his fellow Scot will be a big success and that it is time for disgruntled Villa fans to get behind the controversial appointment.

Supporters protested at Villa Park on Wednesday night but the Manchester United manager is urging those fans to back McLeish and ignore the fact he will arrive from the club's hated neighbours.

"He will be able to assert himself and win over the fans," said Ferguson. "His CV is good. He managed Rangers, he managed Scotland, he won trophies and he's achieved what he has as a manager on limited resources. I think he's done a phenomenal job.

"If you look back 40 years ago, the emotions of supporters were far different then to what they are today. They are very emotional today and they are more personal about their football club. You see many examples of that, particularly Aston Villa in the last few days

"As a football club you can't be swayed from the decisions you have to make. You want to say, 'Look at the manager's cv and look at what he's achieved at other clubs and, for just one minute, forget about the fact he was at Birmingham'.

"At the end of the day, what will count is whether he can do the job for Villa. It doesn't matter whether there are 50 against him or 500 against him or five against him because the experience and the ability he has got, believe me, he will prove that he can do the job.

"In all his jobs he's had to deal with that kind of situation, of making do with what you have and making the best of it. That's a quality."

RON SAUNDERS

Ron Saunders was attractive to the Blues as in 1981 he had taken the Villa to its first Championship success for 70 years in 1981, indeed it was predominantly his team which Tony Barton inherited and took on to win the European Cup a year later. His pedigree was first-class as he had also won the League Cup in 1975 and 1977. He resigned from the Villa Park job and joined Blues on 18 February 1982. As a player he was a hard-shooting centre-forward scoring over 200 goals in 13 years. He was leading goalscorer for six consecutive seasons with Portsmouth and his goals contributed to Pompey's title win in 1962. He remains their third highest goalscorer of all time. He retired from full time football in 1967 to become player-manager of Yeovil Town. He first tasted success at Norwich City getting them to the Division Two title in 1972 achieving promotion to the First Division for the first time in their history. They survived in the top flight and reached the Football League Cup Final losing 1–0 to Tottenham Hotspur. He resigned on 17 November 1973 following a Board Room row after a 3–1 home defeat to Everton. Five days later he accepted the offer to take over at Manchester City and for the second season running he took a team to the League Cup Final only to lose again this time to Wolverhampton Wanderers. He was dismissed three weeks before the end of the season with the club outside of the relegation places on goal average only. The following month he was back in work after being appointed as manager of the Second Division side, Aston Villa. He guided Villa to promotion to the First Division (as runners-up) in his first season as well as winning the League Cup. He became the first manager to guide three different clubs to the League Cup Final in three successive years. He won the League Cup again in 1977 and in 1981 Villa won the First Division title for the first time in 70 years. He resigned from Villa on 9 February 1982 following a disagreement with the Board over his contract. Whilst Villa were mid-table in the First Division they were also in the last eight of the European Cup. Surprisingly he moved straight to Villa's arch-rivals who went down in 1984 but were promoted at the first attempt in May 1985. He walked out on struggling Blues to take charge of West Bromwich Albion on 16 January 1986 but he was unable to stop their relegation to the Second Division and was dismissed in September 1987, his final management appointment.

I was privileged to interview Jim Smith and as part of that meeting I asked him, "*How did your sacking happen?*"

"I was sacked on 13 February 1982 because of our away form we just could not win. My last game, as it turned out, was against West Ham and we were winning 2–1 when, late on, they got the dodgiest penalty ever and we drew 2–2. What I did not know that I was effectively sacked during that game. Ron Saunders who had done a great job at Villa Park, was suddenly available and Jack Wiseman became the main instigator in approaching Ron to take my job. When I got to the ground on the following Monday I surprised to see Keith Coombs' Rolls Royce outside because he had been due to go to the States. My immediate thought was that he was on his way out but of course I could not have been more wrong.

"I was disappointed by the Board's decision because I felt my departure from the Blues was not justified and I feel I was hard done by 'people at Birmingham' and whilst I know exactly who did not 'do me any favours' I am happy that they knew, that I knew what was what!"

In 2006 Saunders was inducted into the Aston Villa Hall of Fame. His win percentage throughout his career was 44.48 per cent – Played 353 games, won 157, drew 98, lost 98.

7

THOUGHTS OF THE BLUENOSES

MICK SHERRY

I have been attending the Blues – Villa games since 1975 and have some wonderful memories of games and battles.

My first encounter was in September 1975 when over 51,000 were at Villa Park with about 15,000 Blues fans situated in the old Witton End that pre-dated the North Stand. The end had no roof and had a grass bank at the top above the terracing. I recall having to queue for tickets for the game on a previous Sunday morning as in those days the majority of the fans were on the terracing and you had to buy the tickets from the turnstiles at Cattell Road entrance rather than the ticket office.

My memories of that day were how wet we all were as it rained and Kenny Burns nearly breaking John Robson's leg. Although we lost 2–1 it was the last time we would lose to Villa for three years. The return leg that season was played in April and a see saw match was won 3–2. The two highlights were a superb Terry Hibbitt volley at the Tilton and the winner was a crack-ing Trevor Francis header at the Railway.

The following season 1976–77 saw Blues win both games 2–1 with the first match at Villa Park in September and the return leg on a Tuesday night in May. I recall both goals at Villa Park were scored at the Holte End and Kenny Burns ran to the front celebrating his goal. The return leg saw two sending's off in separate incidents for Leighton Phillips and Joe Gallagher and Blues recovered from 1–0 down to win 2–1 in the last few minutes. The winner came via a penalty after Andy Gray who was stand-in centre-half fouled Francis who converted the penalty.

The following season 1977–78 saw Blues win both games 1–0 with the first match at Villa Park in October and the return match in February. Keith Bertschin scoring the winner at Villa Park in front of the Blues fans in the new North Stand and Trevor Francis scored in the home match in front of the Villa fans in the Tilton after Jimmy Rimmer had spilled a cross from Tony Towers.

The next match of note was the Boxing Day fixture of 1982 at St Andrew's. Leading up to the game Blues were not particularly in good form and had not won for a month, Villa were the current European Cup holders and went into the game as favourites. The match attracted 43,000, which was a large crowd in that era. The game started well for Blues who went on to secure a 3–0 win very much against the form book. Noel Blake scored the first at the Tilton End in front of the Villa fans after Ian Handysides had hit the post. Blakey had been the subject of some abuse from the Villa fans during the game.

The only two other games of note during the 1980s that I enjoyed were the two wins at Villa Park in March 1986 and August 1987 of 3–0 and 2–0 respectively. The 1986 encounter was notable that Wayne Clarke scored twice at the Holte and was denied a third due to a poor refereeing decision. He rounded Spink and his shot was cleared by the hand of a Villa player that was stood behind the line. It was either a goal or a penalty and the ref played on. Clarke would have netted all three at the Holte End.

There was a lull in league games between the teams in the 1990s due to both sides being in different divisions but it was the first fixture that I looked for when Blues were promoted in 2002. The game in September 2002 was unbelievable. The early goal from Clinton Morrison had set Blues up but Olof Mellberg's throw in that went in under Enckelman's boot was the strangest thing that I have ever seen. The match was the Sky Monday match and was one of best nights I have ever enjoyed at St Andrew's. I also recall in the build up to the game Mellberg had made some derogatory comments that he would hate to ever play for Blues and in the post match interview Steve Bruce acknowledged the comments with a reply to say that, "there is no danger of that happening as based on what I saw tonight Upson and Cunningham are better players and he would not get in the team".

The return match that year was also the Monday night Sky match in March that Blues won 2–0. Both goals scored at the Holte End with Enckelman at fault for the second goal scored by Geoff Horsfield. The match was bad tempered and Villa had two men red carded during the game. Dion

Dublin went first for head butting Robbie Savage followed by Joey Gudjons-son for a stamp on Matthew Upson.

The following season 2003–04 saw Blues win both games 2–1 and 2–0 re-spectively with a helping hand from Thomas Sorenson. At Villa Park in De-cember he let a routine Clinton Morrison shot in and in the return match In March he let an Emile Heskey shot squirm under him. My abiding memory of the home game was the Tilton singing "Tommy, Tommy give us a wave".

PAUL "THE GABBIE CABBIE" COLLINS
A poem from his book *"The Gabbie Cabbies Talk of Fame"*

The Tale of a Divided City

To understand the tale of the divided city, let me take you back many years ago,
When Aston and Birmingham were separate towns, the dividing line was called the "AB Row"
Villa grew out of the Wesleyan Chapel in 1874 from members of a bible club
While at Birmingham a year later, it was cricketers who in the winter months wanted an alternative to going down the pub.

The first league game between them was in 1894 with Villa drawing first blood, 2–1 was the score,
Two years later Aston's lower grounds drew McGregor's visionaries, they changed the name to Villa Park after another two years more.
Birmingham moved to St Andrew's in 1905 and on kicking off a group of gyp-sies, our beloved ground was cursed,

Till legend has it a Bluenose took a brick from the Tilton, planted it in the Holte and now the curse has been reversed.

Villa pioneered the Football League and McGregor was known as the father of the game,
But it's Birmingham who have that family tradition and we carry our city's name.

50 0dd players have swapped sides, the latest export from Blues to Villa was
Alan Curbishley in 1982, and for many of my 45 years I've been hammered
by my mates who follow the claret and blue.
You see, Villa fans have always rubbed our Bluenoses in it; our trophy room is
bare whilst theirs is an awesome sight,

But for most of Villa's achievements the TV wasn't invented and what was recorded, is largely in black and white.

We don't need other influences to stir the hornet's nest, workmates and sib-
lings are at each other's throats till the game has run it's course, For family's
are divided and the rows go on for weeks, sometimes ending in divorce.

So believe me when I say, derby games don't come any bigger than this,
For the losers its hell on earth, as the winners take the piss.
Trust me, there's never any let up and neither is there pity,
That's the inside story of my divided city.

MIKE O'BRIEN

There can be no more pain suffered on a regular basis than that of a Birmingham City and England supporter. Following them home and away knowing
that nine times out of ten there will be far too many lows and not enough highs.

Never mind the likes of Manchester United, Chelsea and Liverpool fans to
name but a few (with half of them never even setting foot in the grounds), who
believe they have a right to success and complain when they finish fifth and
win only one cup. True supporters are the other 95 per cent who typify the
real face of football; win some, lose some, fight tooth and nail for promotion
and the same again to avoid relegation or at best consolidate and try and build
upon what has been achieved and if you reach a major final what a great bonus.

Being a Bluenose is synonymous with this philosophy. You have to hold a
great sense of belief as we battle through adversity on a yearly basis, in the belief that if anything can go wrong it probably will and usually does. We might
not have seen as many great footballers grace St Andrew's as we would have
all liked unless they played for the opposition, but oh how we love a trier who

gives 110 per cent and there have been many more of them over the years. But we are also the club who retains a great sense of humour just look at our fancy dress away days and our great anthem *S...T on the Villa* who can match that.

In the early years I had the huge disappointment of regular relegation battles and of attending every round and reaching the semi-finals then ultimate failures against QPR over two legs (not being able to breathe properly with so many fans shoe-horned into St Andrew's) West Brom, Fulham and that replay and Leeds.

Balanced against that; the promotions, Wembley, the great feeling of achievement at reaching 9th in the premiership. Never have I smiled so much for so long every week. Beating Arsenal in the Carling Cup following J. Wilshere's quote prior to the game, "we haven't decided yet whether C. Fabregas (Captain and unable to play through injury) should pick up the cup". Ever sweeter the victory.

Apart from the usual great memories of some of the games it's funny some of the small incidents that stay with you, of which I have many but I have just listed a few. I started off a babe in arms at St Andrew's; then, as a youngster progressing from being lifted over the turnstiles to later getting into the ground after half-time when the gates were opened. Then paying a couple of bob to get in and to now having to take out a mortgage for a season ticket. I look back now and remember shivering on the Tilton Road, with the lowest attendance's ever and a cup of Bovril to ward off the freezing cold. Getting my programme signed by Kipper Arnold (whoooo I hear you say) and Beau Brummie. Barry Bridges bicycle kicks great goals. Getting struck on the back of the head by a coin thrown from the Arsenal fans, who having climbed over the steel sheeting that served as the fence to the rear of the Tilton Road, proceeded to pelt us with a hail of coins. (They were a lot heavier in the days before decimalisation.) T.F's first game, the 40 yard goals, the four goals in one game. Bob Latchford unnerving the opposing goalkeeper by poleaxing him from the first corner or free kick. The look on their faces always the same as they picked themselves up from the back of the net. Following the promotion team home and away and invariably getting chased back to the train station by opposing fans. Garry Pendry starting a fight to whip up the Blues fans then going on to win the game.

As a lad I went to watch Blues play Sunderland at Roker Park with my uncle who lived in Newcastle, he was also a Newcastle fan. Unfortunately for us both we could only get tickets for the Sunderland end and were surrounded by their fans who directed a tirade of abuse at my beloved team. The vitriol and expletives were only silenced when the false teeth of this fan standing next to me flew out of his mouth onto the terrace (much to our delight). Though this did not last very long as he picked them up wiped them down on his shirt and carried on with the tirade. Which in turn got a lot worse when a lad who continually kept hurling insults at Johnny Vincent – who remember could pin point a 30 yard pass to perfection – finally snapped and on this occasion sent the ball rocketing into him knocking him clean off his feet from about 15 yards. Similar to ten pin bowling. The atmosphere cranked up a notch and was quite electric, but as they won it later, quietened down. Hate to think what would have happened nowadays.

Alongside that are our epic battles with our second city rivals. The euphoria when in 2002–03 we trounced them at Villa Park 20 when D. Dublin flipped and head-butted R. Savage. (who could have been a Blues hero for life if he had been more honest.) Compare him to Gil Merrick who invited me into his home many years before to reminisce about his time at Blues and playing for England and who gave a lot of his memorabilia away to charity events. Or meeting the remaining players of the 1963 final in the legends lounge who were more than happy to have photos taken and sign autographs etc. all night). But I digress, my neighbour at the time was I. Clarkson (Ex Blues Captain also a Fan and a thoroughly decent guy) my other neighbour was a staunch Villa fan. Ian and I decided it was time to celebrate our victory over our rival neighbour. We planned that while he was out we would erect a large banner declaring our great victory to be displayed for all to see on his roof. This we did and to our surprise and delight he did not notice it thinking people passing by were admiring his house. He wasn't amused however when he realised (typical Villa fan) especially when we refused to take it down and as he did not have a ladder got rather perplexed (no sense of humour these Villa fans). Of course after a few days we relented but it just goes to show how the emotions can run so high.

Playing in a school final at 15 and later a senior league final at St Andrew's thus treading in the footsteps of my boyhood heroes was something I always dreamed of when playing football from dusk till dawn at the local park with my mates.

What started off as a bad day 28 July 2005,I had popped into B&Q to make a purchase and upon exiting found somebody had put a brick through the rear windscreen of my estate car, released the cover and pinched a drill. The security wrapped a load of cling film around the tail gate before sending me on my way commenting, you should never park over there mate we always have trouble there with kids. Thinking things couldn't get any worse I drove to St Andrew's and as I came out of the merchandise shop I was lifted off my feet by an unknown force sent tumbling through the air before being un-ceremoniously dumped on to the pavement. Wondering what the hell was happening I valiantly fought my way back up the car park which seemed to take an eternity, through torrential rain with tree branches, dirt and bottles swirling around my head. Finally managing to get to the relative safety of my car which was bouncing all over the place with the cling film flying like a flag. I looked up at the blackened sky to see quite a number of large steel sheets flying through the air and coming towards me like something out of Harry Potter before crashing and skidding along the tarmac with some embedding themselves under my car wheels before slamming into the rear fence. Total mayhem then utter calm in a matter of minutes. Later that evening I watched in disbelief on TV the destructive trail through Birmingham from a tornado with winds of 150 mph and heard that the steel sheeting had been lifted off nearby roofs. I was left wondering why they had slid under and around the car not into it or through the front screen. Of course it was because I was a Bluenose!!!!!

JOHN BILL

Once a bluenose always a blue nose! Looking back I suppose it was inevitable that I would become a supporter of the men in blue. My mother was born and lived the first 14 years of her life a stone's throw from St Andrew's. My grand-father (her father) was a lifetime bluenose and spent many an evening in the days before the war, drinking in the local pubs with the players and ex-players of the day. Often in these days when a player retired from being a professional footballer, he ended up either running or owning a Public House!

At 14 years old Mom and family were moved out, en bloc, together, with the many other families from Bordesley Park Road, to Highters Heath. Most of them (who still remained close) either supported the Blues or the Baggies.

My father was not a football fan and so it came to pass that my very first visit to a football ground as a boy in my last year at Junior School, was a match on 14 January 1961 at Villa Park! Aston Villa vs Bristol Rovers, Football League Division Two, which Villa won 4–1. I went with a friend from School, whose father was disillusioned enough to be an avid Villa fan.

It took me another three years to sufficiently recover from this experience, enough to be able to go to where my heart was obviously leading me, across the city to the mecca of football, St Andrew's. This time under my own steam, with a mate from secondary school. At last I felt at home. However, it was not all plain sailing from there on in. In 1966, if you wanted to see any preliminary rounds of the World Cup Finals, as I did, I ending up once again at that ridiculous painted ground in Aston, watching the likes of Spain, Argentina and West Germany (well at least they did not play in those horrendous colours!)

This experience turned out to be not all bad, however, as through a ballot, I ended up at Wembley in July 1966, watching England beat West Germany in the Final, 4–2, to record our only every World Cup trophy win.

Anyway, back to the blues, from 1964 through to the early 1980s I was a regular visitor to St Andrew's (and many away matches too) during which time, we notched up some memorable wins over Aston Villa in what was then the First Division. I recall a memorable 3–0 victory at St Andrew's in the first meeting between the sides, following the Villa's fluky European Cup triumph in 1982.

As the two teams then went their separate ways, other than the odd League Cup match here and there, there was a gap of some 15 years, before the next eagerly awaited league derby following Blues triumphant promotion to the Premier League in 2002!

I was lucky enough to be sitting in a box belonging to a client at St Andrew's, when our eleven men in blue, plus Peter Enkelman in the Villa goal, set out with a point to prove; i.e. who should be the top dog in the second city. What a return to the top flight it was, with the Blues winning both derby's 3–0 at St Andrews and then 2–0 at Villa Park.

Yes, at times, there have been the odd lucky wins for Aston Villa since, but it took them until the 2005–06 season to record their first win in the Premiership derby.

As a lifelong Birmingham City fan, there has not been that much to rejoice about (with the exception of again finding myself at Wembley watching a memorable win over Arsenal). Our only major trophy wins have been winning the Carling Cup/League Cup twice and guess who we beat to record our first victory? Yes it was Aston Villa.

DES PONSONBY

Where to start! I was Managing Director of a medium sized Haulage Company which was turning over about £6mill per annum back in the early 2000s. We had huge cash flow issues brought on because we had expanded into various marketplaces but had totally lost our ability to generate profit. In that fateful month of September 2002, my business was in tatters and I knew that nothing could stop us lurching into administration. On the actual day of the first Blues v Villa top flight derby for 16 years, I spent it watching our trucks, trailers and premises being reclaimed by a firm of administrators. I felt lower than a snakes belly, In the previous May, Blues had won the Play-Off Final against Norwich City at the Millennium stadium and all Blues fans were buzzing, however my business problems had taken precedence over the first few games back in the top flight and in a way I was dreading Villa kicking our butt and leaving us in our usual position of 'poor relations' to our up market neighbours.

However that performance from Blues who out ran, out worked and out gunned Villa became the focal point for me to throw away my woes and use it as the trigger to achieve success again. I always recall arriving at St Andrew's about 15 minutess before kick-off and immediately thinking, this atmosphere is like the 1970s when the ground was predominantly standing!

Both sets of fans were baying at each other, Graham Taylor (Villa manager) had foolishly come out and said that our promotion just guaranteed them six easy points that season! Blues started off well and Clinton Morrison put us ahead just before half-time with a sweet finish, but early in the second half came the turning point, Vassell slotted one into the Railway End but it was chalked offside, from then on Blues totally took over, Robbie Savage won everything in midfield while Geoff Horsfield terrorised Villa's two international centre-backs, the unforgettable moment when Villa's 'Keeper Peter Enkleman became a member of Blues Legends Pantheon by allowing a throw in to brush his foot and trickle into the net. The crowd (well the blue majority) went mental, noise levels were at fever pitch, I've never known an atmosphere like it before or since, the game was topped off when The Horse tripped round his two dejected markers to slot home...3–0.

Blues were not only back but back on top, I recall the next morning thinking how Steve Bruce had revived the club in just a few months and thinking I can do that! The next day I gathered round me the people who I felt were up for the challenge and we literally sat down with a clean sheet of paper and said right this is the way forward. Now a decade on we are a profitable £10 million company who totally reinvented the way we work, when I look back I think it was the effort and enthusiasm of those players in Blues shirts that night that convinced me that anything is achievable if you want it enough! Keep Right On!

ERIC BIGNELL – SOLIHULL
THE CASE OF THE VANISHING VILLA FANS

It was season 1948–49 and the venue was Villa Park. I attended the match with five Villa supporters who agreed between them to buy me a tea if Blues won. In return, I would buy each of them a team if Villa won. With 15 minutes to go and Blues leading 3–0 the five said Villa fans mysteriously vanished and missed Joe Rutherford hauling down Harold Bodle for the most blatant penalty never given. I'm still waiting for the tea!

P. THOMPSON, GILLINGHAM
VICTORY AT VILLA PARK

My best memory from supporting the Blues goes back to the 1967–68 season and took place at Villa Park of all places!

I had left school and my first job was with the son of one of the Villa directors. He was Villa through and through and knew that I was a true blue. Even so he would always offer me tickets for Villa Park, which I declined.

In due course, we were due to play at Villa Park but I felt awkward about asking for a ticket having refused the offer previously. Five minutes before the finishing time on the Friday afternoon I received a summons from the manager. This normally meant a rollicking, so I approached the office with some trepidation, especially as I received a curt 'Come on' in answer to my knock on the door. He then made me sweat even more by shuffling papers on his desk. Finally, he said, "You haven't asked me for tickets?" I began to explain that I didn't like to ask as I had always refused to date, but he cut my explanation short. He then handed me an envelope containing two complimentary tickets to the Directors' Box.

On my way home I stopped off at a friend's house and asked if he fancied watching the big game from the Directors' Box. He began to laugh until I showed him the tickets when his jaw dropped. The following day two young lads sat at the back of the Directors' Box determined to enjoy themselves whatever the result. However, we lost some of the gloss when Villa scored, nevertheless Blues did us proud by equalising, but still went in at half-time on the wrong end of a 2–1 scoreline. The second half was a different story as Blues were rampant. What a day – two very happy teenage lads had watched the match at Villa Park from the Directors' Box for free with a final score of Aston Villa 2 Birmingham City 4

JOSEPH DONOHUE DORSET

7 October 1967 Aston Villa 2 Blues 4. A 50,000 crowd with the Holte End packed to the rafters with Blues fans in the days before segregation. We were all wearing scarves, hats and waving banners – the noise was amazing!

Tommy Docherty led his Villa side out in front of the Holte End with the manager trying to stir up the crowd. I'll never forget the look on his face when he realised that the Holte End was 80 per cent full of Blues fans. Not long before derby day he predicted that Villa would rule Birmingham and we slaughtered them – magnificent

PHIL JONES CORNWALL

My best memory from supporting Blues is one with 11 good reasons. Herriot, Murray, Martin, Wylie, Foster, Beard, Bridges, Vincent, Pickering, Vowden and Hockey – although it is a difficult choice between Martin and Green for that position. I believe that team of 1967–68 was one of our finest ever with so many memorable matches to savour. Not only was it my first season as a fan on the terraces but it was my first derby at Villa Park and what a pulsating match that was! 1–0 down, 2–1 down and eventual 4–2 winners – one of the best Blues v Villa derbies.

PAUL FULFORD

Diehard Bluenose Paul wrote in the *Evening Mail* 17/09/2002,

"16 YEARS OF PAIN BURIED ON A NIGHT TO REMEMBER"

There's no mistaking Blues and Villa fans today as the reality of last night's second city clash sinks in. The blue half of the city are the ones sporting smiles as broad as the Coventry Road as they celebrate their emphatic win over their bitterest rivals. Sixteen years our of the top-flight, sixteen years since the teams met in the league, sixteen years of under-achievement.

That was the legacy that was forgotten as first Clinton Morrison scored, the Villa conceded a bizarre own goal and finally Geoff Horsfield slotted in a third.

There were excruciatingly tense moments in between as Villa rattled the crossbar and had a goal disallowed, but the night belonged to Blues.

"Can we play you every week?" sang the Blues supporters, taunting the fast-diminishing enclave of Villa fans in the Railway End.

"There's only one Graham Taylor," they chanted as still more Villa fans slipped out of the ground.

A 1–0 win would have left us Blues fans defending our right to the three points. Two-nil would have left us crowing. But 3–0? That was the stuff of dreams

There's a temptation to be magnanimous after such a resounding victory, but many minds turned back to the jibes directed at Blues by Villa fans after crushingly embarrassing cup defeats by Altrincham and Kidderminster.

So we clapped chanted and danced with delight as the hurt of spending 16 years as undisputed underdogs was exorcised.

Children who weren't born the last time Blues were in the top flight sang alongside parents old enough to know better. The battle anthem *Keep Right On To The End Of The Road* echoed round St Andrew's.

Pouring out of the ground, Blues fans wreathed in smiles. Some chuckled out loud. Many made mobile phone calls or sent text messages. And today the

Blues fans were still relishing their moment of long-awaited joy...while Villa fans were already praying for revenge in March's return fixture.

KARIM ADAB

I feel that in a physical, entertaining spectacle the Blues/Villa derby games show the others what local pride ought to really mean. Bar everything but the Sectarian nonsense which exists north of the border, the white-hot atmosphere of the Birmingham encounter eclipses any other local tiff within these shores. Forget the powder-puff affairs in London, phoney Scouse bonhomie and showboating Manchester events – our derbies reveal glimpses of the oft-forgotten quintessential English game: sturm und drang, blood and thunder, game after game after game.

DARREN PORTER – SKYDAZ

What derby games are all about and what they mean to us fans: Passion, Commitment, Fanaticism, Determination, Belligerence.

55 BIASED FACTS AND FIGURES

1. The clubs first met on 27 September 1879, when Birmingham City was called Small Heath Alliance. The game, a friendly fixture, was played on a pitch at Small Heath's Muntz Street ground, described by the Villa players as, "only suitable for pot-holing" and a "paddy field". The game finished 1–0 – recorded as "one goal and a disputed goal to nil" to the home side. (Author's Note: Villa's mentality of blaming everything except itself when they suffer a defeat was established on this day?)

2. FA Cup Semi-Final 1886 – after beating Villa it was recorded that each Blues player received 2/6d – one shilling for a cab to the ground and 1/6d for a meal.

3. Friendly 1889–90, won 4–0 at home.

4. Friendly 1890–91, won 4–0 away.

5. Friendly 1895–96, won 2–1 away.

6. June 1896 – First record transfer fee for a player from Blues to Villa was established by Fred Wheldon for the princely sum of £350.

7. Friendly 1896–97, won 2–1 at home in Billy Walton's benefit game.

8. Lord Mayor of Birmingham's Charity Cup Competition 1904 – joint holders with Aston Villa as the game was abandoned after 50 minutes.

9. The Blues' first ever Football League win over Villa came in September 1905 – 2–0 at Muntz Street.

10. Blues' first away victory was recorded on 20 January 1906.

11. First win over Villa at St Andrew's was 19 January 1907, winning 3–2 in the First Division.

12. Lord Mayor of Birmingham's Charity Cup Competition 1906–07, won 4–0 in front of 12,000 spectators.

13. Lord Mayor of Birmingham's Charity Cup Competition 1907–08, won 5–2 in front of 10,000 spectators. Jack Dorrington saved two penalties from Villa's Harry Hampton.

14. Staffordshire Senior Cup – in 1914–15, Blues won 1–0 in the Final watched by 3,000 fans.

15. Lord Mayor of Birmingham's Charity Cup Competition 1918–19, won 4–1 in front of 6,116 spectators.

16. Friendly 1918–19, won 2–1 away for County FA Fund.

17. Lord Mayor of Birmingham's Charity Cup Competition 1933–34, won 2–0 in front of 10,876 spectators.

18. Lord Mayor of Birmingham's Charity Cup Competition 1934–35, won 2–1 in front of 6,334 spectators.

19. Lord Mayor of Birmingham's Charity Cup Competition 1935–36, won 4–2 in front of 5,504 spectators.

20. Blues went six games undefeated on two occasions: 8 March 1933 to 23 November 1935 and 16 September 2002 to 20 March 2005.

21. Friendly 1939–40, won 2–1 in Harry Hibbs' Testimonial match.

22. Friendly 1940–41, won 2–1 at home.

23. First game in second division 7 October 1967, Blues won 2–1 at Villa Park.

24. Largest winning margin for Blues was 4 goals on 21 September 1968.

25. Blues won five games in a row from 3 April 1976 to 25 February 1978.

26. Birmingham Senior Cup 1982–83, won 1–0, Ian Handysides scored in front of a crowd of 11,763.

Blues win Birmingham Senior Cup 1982-83

27. Birmingham Senior Cup 1995–96, won 2–0, Jason Bowen and Ricky Otto scoring with an attendance of 1,773.

28. First game in Premiership was 16 September 2002 beating the Villa 3–0 at home in front of 29,505 spectators.

29. The last Birmingham City league victory over Aston Villa was on 20 March 2005, when Blues won 2–0 at St Andrew's.

30. Season 2010–11 season resulted in the first Blues win since 2005, as they beat Villa 2–1 in the League Cup Quarter Final on 1 December 2010.

31. Blues goal scorers in the Victories against the Villa:
4. Bridges and Leek.
3. Francis, Bradford, Mounteney, Briggs, Harris F., Harris J.
2. Jones, Green, Crosbie, Stewart, Kinsey, Brown E., Jackson, Vowden, Burns, Hibbitt, Handysides, Clarke, Morrison, Horsfield.
1. Dougherty, Eyre, Rawson, Clark, Islip, Mills, Grosvenor, Guest, Brown J., Bodle, Murphy, Neal, Astall, Orritt, Lynn, Bloomfield, Hellawell, Beard, Greenhoff, Vincent, Summerill, Connolly, Bertschin, Blake, Ferguson, Stevenson, Gayle, Rees, Whitton, Lazaridis, Dunn, Heskey, Gray. Own Goal: Enckelman.

32. Who played in the Victories against the Villa:
7. Bradford.
6. Crosbie, Smith T., Beard, Page, Calderwood.
5. Francis, Hibbitt, Tremelling, Jones J.
4. Wigmore, Green B., Mounteney, Liddell, Barton, Lynn, Hellawell, Hennessey, Harris J., Auld, Green C., Gallagher, Johnson D., Morrison, Cunningham.
3. Robinson, Glover, Beer, Jones W., McClure, Harvey, Harris F., Briggs, Hibbs, Morrall, Want, Styles, Burns, Roberts B., Savage, Clapham, Upson, Lazaridis, Carter, Merrick, Schofield, Hall, Watts, Neal, Astall, Wylie, Herriot, Leek, Vincent, Vowden, Latchford D.
2. Stokes, Dougherty, Cornan, Harper, Ashurst, Clark, Dale, Womack, Barkas, Leslie, Booton, Stoker, Calladine, Clemence, Taylor M., Heskey, Gray, Jones G., Connolly, Pendrey, Montgomery, Towers, Howard, Broadhurst, Bertschin, Dillon, Coton, Van Den Hauwe, Stevenson, Blake, Handysides, Hagan, Kuhl, Hopkins, Bremner, Whitton, Vaesen, Kenna, Devlin, Horsfield, Roberts, Jennings, Green K., Kinsey, Brown

E., Murphy, Larkin, Sissons, Withers, Foster, Bridges, Pickering, Hockey, Martin R., Kendall.

1. Wilcox, Field, Hartwel,l Anderson, Dorrington, Corbett, Kerns, Tickle, Bluff, Drake, Eyre, Roulson, Barratt, Hampton, Foxall, Dawes, Rawson, Lane, Cringan, Islip, Scriven, Hunter, Linley, Russell, Randle, Mills, Hicks, Grosvenor, Gregg, Curtis, Hubbard, Moffatt, Mangnall, Guest, Dugarry, Tebily, Dunn, Anderton, Panadiani, Melchiot, Nafti, Needham, Hatton, Rathbone, Emmanuel, Fox, Langan, Harford, Ferguson, Curbishley, Gayle, McCarrick, Halsall, Godden, Dicks, Williams, Overson, Kennedy, Rees, Wigley, Seaman, Ranson, Garton, Clarke, Wright, Grainger, Purse, John, Cisse, Powell, Huighes, Clack, Trigg, Hughes, Dearson, Meacock, White, Phillips, Brown J., Duckhouse, Mitchell, Berry, Stewart, Dougall, Bodle, Govan, Farmer, Hooper, Allen, Gordon, Jackson, Taylor B., Orritt, Stubbs, Murray, Robinson, Greenhoff, Summerill.

33. Harry Hibbs was the only footballer to receive a testimonial during World War II against Aston Villa in April 1940. "One war-time fixture at bomb-scarred St Andrew's when the crowd was pitifully slender saw Harry Hibbs make his farewell for Birmingham in a specially arranged game." Hibbs had begun and ended his illustrious career against the old enemy. On May 20 1924, he appeared for the first time in the Lord Mayor of Birmingham's Charity Cup. His swan song was head on April 13 1940, when Blues won 2–1.

34. Joe Gallagher was sent off against the Villa on 10 May 1977.

35. Paul Tait was sent off against the Villa on 6 October 1993 in Second Leg of 1993–94 League Cup second round at Villa Park.

36. John Cornforth was sent off against the Villa on 8 May 1996 – Birmingham Senior Cup Final at St Andrew's.

37. Ian Jones was sent off against the Villa on 8 May 1996 – Birmingham Senior Cup Final at St Andrew's.

38. Paul Peschisolido was sent off against the Villa on 8 May 1996 – Birmingham Senior Cup Final at St Andrew's.

39. During the Second World War Blues played the Villa in 1942–43 three times, winning once at home 2–1 (although all home games were played at Villa Park) on 28 November 1942.

40. During the Second World War Blues played the Villa in 1943–44 twice, winning once at Home 2–1 on 26 February 1944.

41. During the Second World War Blues played the Villa in 1944–45 four times, winning once at home 3–2 on 7 October 1944.

42. During the Second World War Blues played the Villa in 1945–46 twice, winning once at home 3–1 on 19 January 1946.

43. In the final match of the 1945–46 season Blues had to win away at Luton to beat Villa to the League (South) Championship. They beat them 3–0 with goals from Frank Bodle, a Frank Mitchell spot-kick and a third from Jock Mulraney. Blues had 61 points the same as the Villa but our goal difference of 96–45 was better than 106–58 by 0.206 of a goal.

44. Blues have had five England Full International goalkeepers amassing 51 appearances: Dan Tremelling (1), Harry Hibbs (25), Gil Merrick (23), Ben Foster (1), and Jack Butland (1), at the end of the 2012–13 season. Whilst Villa have had six England Full International goalkeepers they only had an aggregate number of appearances of 18: Bill George (3), Sam Hardy (7), Ben Olney (2), Nigel Spink (1), David James (3), and Scott Carson (2).

45. Blues recorded 18 consecutive home wins in 1945–46 on their way to winning the Football League (South) Championship.

46. Blues doubled the admission price for their home FA Cup tie against Villa in March 1901 – only 18,000 turned up against the expected 25,000 but the receipts were higher than normal.

47. Joe Bradford made most appearances for Blues in derby games against the Villa – a total of 23 – scoring most goals as well – eight.

48. In August 2003 David Sullivan broached the possibility of a ground share with Aston Villa – How out of touch with the fans can you get! Although in season 2013–14 he would be welcomed back with open arms.

49. A crowd of 63,820 saw the Aston Villa v Birmingham League South game at Villa Park in January 1946.

50. In the late 19th century – Chris Charsley (1890), Ted Devey (1895), James Elliott (1896), and Billy Walton (1897) enjoyed testimonial games against the Villa.

51. In the 1980s and 1990s – Joe Gallagher (1981,) Kevan Broadhurst (1986), and John Frain (1996) enjoyed testimonial games against the Villa, the latter in May when 8,000 fans paid £5,000.

52. In 1980 Ron Saunders enjoyed a testimonial game against the Villa which was held in the May at Villa Park and Blues triumphed 3–2.

53. Bob Brocklebank who managed Blues from January 1949 and October 1954 was born in Finchley on 23 May 1908 and played as an inside-forward with Finchley Boys initially and then Finchley in August 1925. He played for Aston Villa from May 1929 until moving to Burnley in March 1936. After retiring as a player in August 1945, he managed Chesterfield (September 1945 to January 1949) after Blues he was with

West Bromwich Albion as Coach/Scout (October 1954 to March 1955) returning to management with Hull City (March 1955 to May 1961) his final managerial role was with Bradford City from May 1961 to October 1964 when he retired to Brixham in South Devon where he died on 3 September 1981.

54. At the time of the Carson Yeung takeover the *SUN* newspaper did an article of the financial status of the Premier League sides at the time. Aston Villa were recorded as having a NET DEBT of £72.26m whilst Blues had NET FUNDS of £2.41m.

55. Karren Brady in her *SUN* article posed the following question: Aston Villa. They may be rivals but Everton and Liverpool fans aren't enemies outside of football. Not true of many Blues and Villa fans in Brum and I wish it were. If only they could share a joke – say, Peter Enckelman's hilarious own goal or Robbie Savage's Richard III haircut. This question demonstrates Ms Brady's poor sense of humour and after being at the club since 1992–93 no true understanding of the relationship between the two sets of fans!! This is partly evidenced by the incident when she and Terry Cooper had lunch with Doug Ellis. He introduced Ron Atkinson to Karren, and upon seeing the team sheet she said "Oh, how lovely, your son plays." "No," said Ron, "Dalian is one of my players." Terry Cooper's head was in his hands.

ODDS 'N SODS

NUMBER ONE

On a 1922 Cigarette card issued by Gallagher Limited of Belfast and London: Series – Footballers No 14 of a series of 100.

1922 Cigarette Card

Birmingham v Aston Villa

Dan Tremelling, the Birmingham goalkeeper, has here rushed out to fist the ball away during an onslaught by the Aston Villa forwards. He has pushed the ball off the head of Cook, the Villa forward. Two other Villa forwards, Walker and Beresford are on the right of the picture.

NUMBER TWO

Garry Thompson recalls:

"I wasn't allowed to celebrate that win at Blues in December 1987. Me and Gary Shaw went into town for a few celebratory drinks. We went to a wine bar just off Broad Street and then on to a night club. There followed a bit of banter with a bouncer but then he told us that he couldn't guarantee our safety. "Do your-selves a favour and go home," he said. I couldn't believe it. There we were, on the back of a massive win and just trying to enjoy the moment. And there was this guy telling us we weren't allowed in because there were five Bluenoses sat in a corner inside that wanted to kick things off. I shouted over to them, something like, "Come on chaps it's only a game" and I was still keen to go inside. But when I looked around Shaw had already done his about-turn. And that was it. We were escorted from the premises. And after such a big win I ended up going home early! And that hurts even now. *Evening Mail;* 19 March 2005.

NUMBER THREE
ELEVEN PLAYERS BORN IN ASTON, SIGNED BY BLUES WHO FAILED
TO MAKE A MARK

Edward Bailey	1 appearance
Francis Banks	3 appearances
Fred Banks	1 appearance
Sam Bellamy	1 appearance
James Bye	2 appearances
Joe Fountain	3 appearances
Walter Gittins	5 appearances
Albert Lindon	7 appearances
Joe Taylor	3 appearances
Archie Vale	2 appearances
Harry Williams	1 appearance

NUMBER FOUR
It was Christmas 2006 when Blues decided to present to their corporate guests a Club Diary for 2007. A great idea, well received by the recipients but what a shock they had when they turned to the page headed "Club Honours". Instead of recording the Leyland Daf and Auto Windscreen's Shield triumphs the tome stated quite clearly that not only had we won seven League Championships and seven FA Cups we had also been victorious in Europe! What had happened? Well the problem was within the Marketing department where they had failed to adequately check the proof when it had come from the printers, as it was a

concept whereby the basic diary was "personalised" to suit the ordering club. As was the style of the club during the Brady/Deakin era the printers took the blame and a junior member of the marketing team lost their job. The only good thing to come out of this situation would have been the faces of the corporate guests at Villa Park if they got a Blues' version!!!

NUMBER FIVE

Penalty Kicks came into the game in 1891 and typically it took Blues three years to be awarded a spot kick against Bolton Wanderers in September 1894. Fred Wheldon (who joined Aston Villa two years later) missed although we won the game 2–0. Wheldon dismissed any conspiracy theories a month later when he scored Blues' first penalty kick conversion against the Villa. Whilst on the subject of penalty kicks, Stan Lynn had an incredible record of converting penalty chances, including scoring a penalty for Blues against the Villa and one for Villa against the Blues!

NUMBER SIX

The record for the youngest ever full-back pairing in the Football League still belongs to Blues, when both Cyril Trigg and Billy Hughes made their debuts at the age of eighteen against the Villa in March 1936.

NUMBER SEVEN

We know Aston Villa claim to have fans of the status of Prince William, David Cameron, Nigel Kennedy and Tom Hanks and we would counter with Jasper Carrott, Jeff Lynne, Roy Wood and Ali Campbell amongst our ranks of celebrities that love the Blues. But I doubt whether Villa can claim to have a celebrity supporter that actually sits in the stands (that still does not make sense!) like Colin Buchanan. On several occasions fans in the Kop Stand in section 22/24 have done "double takes" at this familiar face from the TV programme *"Dalziel and Pascoe"* sits alone amongst the fans as one of us! Kop Stand Section 26. Although born in Edinburgh, Colin visits Birmingham regularly as the series is filmed in Brum although the implied location is Yorkshire, and has become a Bluenose. He can also be found in The Plough at Harborne during his off-duty hours.

Another proud Brummie actor is David Harewood. The 47 year-old former Washwood Heath Comprehensive pupil has been nominated as best supporting actor in the *Entertainment Weekly* magazine awards for his role *in Homeland*. He starred in the TV show as CIA counter-terrorism director David Estes. He has a star on Birmingham's Walk of Stars.

HOMELAND is an American drama-thriller television series based on the Israel series *Hatufim* (English title: Prisoners of War) created by Gideon Raff. The series stars Claire Daines as Carrie Mathison, a C.I.A. officer with bipolar disorder and Damian Lewis as Nicholas Brody a United States Marine Corps Scout Sniper. Mathison has come to believe that Brody, who was held captive by al-Qaeda as a prisoner-of-war was "turned" by the enemy and now threatens the U.S.A.

NUMBER EIGHT

In 1942 The Main Stand was destroyed by fire. Attempts to quell the flames sadly, and some would say in typical Blues fashion, failed when a member of the fire services used petrol instead of water. Aston Villa offered Birmingham the use of Villa Park. Was the offer accepted?

NUMBER NINE

In 1897 Small Heath bought a stand from Aston Villa at a cost of £90 and placed it behind one of the goals at Muntz Street. Even in Victorian times spectator comfort was a prime concern of The Blues.

NUMBER TEN

For Christmas 2007 Blues released a DVD entitled " Birmingham City – The 250 Greatest Goals"

The selection began in December 1969 and featured these goals against the Villa:

Date	Goal Scorer
18/9/1976	John Connolly
31/03/1984	Byron Stevenson
31/03/1984	Howard Gayle

16/09/2002	Clinton Morrison
16/09/2002	Geoff Horsfield
16/09/2002	Peter Enckelman (own goal)
03/03/2003	Geoff Horsfield
03/03/2003	Stan Lazaridis
22/02/2004	Stern John
22/02/2004	Mikael Forssell
12/12/2004	Clinton Morrison
20/03/2005	Julian Gray
20/03/2005	Emile Heskey

10

PIONEERS OF COMPETITIVE EUROPEAN CLUB FOOTBALL

Although Villa have played to date 85 games in European Club competitions since 1975–76 season none of this could have happened without the pioneering spirit of their fiercest rivals. After Villa rejected the invitation to form a combined Birmingham XI, Blues went it alone!

Competitive European competition began in the mid 1950s with the IN-TER-CITIES FAIRS CUP The competition was played between 1955 and 1971 as the name suggests it was set up to promote international trade fairs. The competition was initially only open to teams from cities that hosted trade fairs and where these teams finished in their domestic leagues had no relevance.

The first competition was to be held over two seasons to avoid clashes with national leagues fixtures. because it was also intended to coincide with trade fairs, it ran over into a third year. It commenced in 1955 and finished in 1958. The first English participant in the initial competition was a representative side from London, imaginatively entitled LONDON XI. Unlike its opposition it was a truly representative side with representatives from all senior London clubs but the BARCELONA XI comprised of ten regular Barcelona players and a token representative from ESPANOL. Not surprisingly BARCELONA XI won handsomely 8–2 on aggregate.

The next tournament featured club sides only, making BIRMINGHAM CITY the first-ever English club side to participate in a European Club competition.

Blues' involvement in competitive European football spans five decades following its involvement in the Inter-Cities Fairs Cup and its recently sojourn into the Europa League competition.

The UEFA Europa League was established for the 2009–10 season after being known as the UEFA Cup since 1971. Clubs qualify based on their performance in their national leagues and cup competitions. For UEFA football records purposes, the UEFA Cup and UEFA Europa League are considered to be the same competition with the change of name being regarded as a simple rebrand of the competition. In 1999 the UEFA Cup Winners' Cup was abolished and merged with the UEFA Cup. The UEFA Cup was preceded by the Inter-Cities Fairs Cup which was a European football competition played between 1955 and 1971. The competition grew from 11 teams during the first cup (1955-58) to 64 teams by the last competition which was played in 1970–71. The competition had become so important on the European football scene that in the end it was taken over by UEFA and re-launched the following season as the UEFA Cup.

The competitors include the runners-up of domestic leagues, the winners of domestic cup competitions, clubs eliminated in the third qualifying round of the UEFA Champions League and the third placed teams at the end of the group phase of the UEFA Champions League. Also admitted are three Fair Play representatives and winners of some domestic league cup competitions.

Blues achievements in these early days were significant:
1956-58 – Semi-Finalist
1958-60 – Finalist
1960-61 – Finalist
1961-62 – Reached Round 2

The details are as follows:

1956–1958

Played in four groups, the top club in each group qualifying for the semi-finals

Group B Table

	P	W	D	L	F	A	Pts
Blues	4	3	1	0	6	1	7
Internazionale	4	2	1	1	6	2	5
Dinamo Zagreb	4	0	0	4	0	9	0

Internazionale Milan Team Group 1956-58

Team Sheet - Dinamo Zagreb 1956-58

Group B Results

Match	Date	Venue	Opposition	Score	Crowd
A	16/05/56	Away	Internazionale (Italy)	0–0	8,000
B	21/05/56	Away	Zagreb Select (Yugoslavia)	0–1	12,000
C	03/12/56	Home	Zagreb Select (Yugoslavia)	3–0	40,144
D	17/04/57	Home	Internazionale (Italy)	2–1	30,791

Len Boyd travelled alone due to his fear of flying; he caught the ferry to mainland Europe and travelled by train across France to Italy.

Group B Appearances and Goals

A	B	C	D
MERRICK	MERRICK	MERRICK	MERRICK
BADHAM	BADHAM	FARMER	HALL
GREEN	ALLEN	ALLEN	GREEN
WATTS	BOYD	WATTS	WATTS
NEWMAN	NEWMAN	GREEN	SMITH
WARMINGTON	WARHURST	WARHURST	WARHURST
COX	LANE	COX	ASTALL
KINSEY	KINSEY	ORRITT (1)	KINSEY
BROWN	BROWN (1)	BROWN (1)	BROWN(2)
MURPHY	MURPHY	MURPHY (1)	MURPHY
GOVAN	GOVAN	GOVAN	GOVAN

SEMI-FINAL First Leg

- 23 October 1957 v Barcelona (Spain), Home 4–3 Attendance: 30,791
- MERRICK, FARMER, ALLEN, LARKIN, SMITH, WATTS, ASTALL, ORRITT (1), BROWN (1), NEAL, MURPHY (2).

SEMI-FINAL Second Leg
- 13 November 1957 v Barcelona (Spain), Away 1–0 Attendance: 60,000
- MERRICK, HALL, ALLEN, LARKIN, SMITH, NEAL, ASTALL, KINSEY, BROWN, MURPHY, GOVAN

After two legs the aggregate score was 4–4 requiring a replay to be played at St. Jacob Stadium, Basle, Switzerland.

SEMI-FINAL Replay
- 26 November 1957 v Barcelona (Spain), Neutral 1–2 Attendance: 20,000
- MERRICK, HALL, FARMER, WATTS, SMITH, NEAL, ASTALL, ORRITT, BROWN, MURPHY (1), GOVAN

1958–60

Round 1 First Leg
- 14 October 1958 v Cologone Select (Germany), Away 2–2 Attendance 12,000
- MERRICK, HALL, GREEN, WATTS, SISSONS, NEAL (1), HOOPER (1), GORDON, BROWN, ORRITT, MURPHY.

Round 1 Second Leg
- 11 November 1958 v Cologne Select Home 2–0 Attendance 20,266
- MERRICK, HALL, ALLEN, WATTS, SMITH, NEAL, HOOPER, GORDON, BROWN, LARKIN (1), TAYLOR (1).
- WON 4–2 ON AGGREGATE.

Round 2 First Leg
- 6 May 1959 v Dinamo Zagreb (Yugoslavia), Home 1–0 Attendance 21,411
- SCHOFIELD, FARMER, ALLEN, WATTS, SISSONS, NEAL, HOOPER, GORDON, STUBBS, LARKIN (1), TAYLOR.

Round 2 Second Leg
- 24 May 1959 v Dinamo Zagreb, Away 3–3 Attendance 50,000
- SCHOFIELD, FARMER, ALLEN, WATTS, SMITH, NEAL, ASTALL, GORDON, STUBBS, LARKIN (2), HOOPER (1).
- WON 4–3 ON AGGREGATE

Union St.Gilloise Team Group 1959

Semi-Final First Leg
- 7 October 1959 v Union St Gilloise (Belgium), Away 4–2 Attendance 20,000
- MERRICK, SISSONS, FARMER, WATTS, SMITH, NEAL, HOOPER (1), GORDON (1), ORRITT (1), BARRETT (1), TAYLOR.

Semi-Final Second Leg
- 11 November 1959 v Union St. Gilloise (Belgium), Home 4–2 Attendance 14,152
- SCHOFIELD, FARMER, ALLEN, WATTS, SMITH, LARKIN (1), HELLAWELL, BARRETT, GORDON (2), HOOPER (1 penalty), TAYLOR.
- WON – 8–4 ON AGGREGATE

OFFICIAL PROGRAMME

INTER-CITIES FAIRS CUP COMPETITION — FINAL TIE — 1st LEG

BIRMINGHAM CITY

v.

C. F. BARCELONA

TUESDAY, 29th MARCH, 1960
ST. ANDREW'S GROUND, BIRMINGHAM
KICK-OFF 7-15 P.M.

PRICE 6D.

Programme 29th March 1960

Final First Leg

- 29 March 1960 v Barcelona (Spain), Home 0–0 Attendance 40,524
- SCHOFIELD, FARMER, ALLEN, WATTS, SMITH, NEAL, ASTALL, GORDON, WESTON, ORRITT, HOOPER

Final Second Leg

- 4 May 1960 v Barcelona (Spain), Away 1–4 Attendance 75,000
- SCHOFIELD, FARMER, ALLEN, WATTS, SMITH, NEAL, ASTALL, GORDON, WESTON, MURPHY, HOOPER (1)

Match Report from *Daily Mirror*, Thursday, 5 May 1960:

BRUM' GET A FINAL HIDING

Birmingham were crushed here tonight in this second leg of the Inter-Cities Fairs Cup Final. After holding the clever Spaniards to 0–0 in the first leg at Birmingham three weeks ago, they were hopelessly outclassed. Barcelona, in fact, won the match in the first six minutes with goals from centre-forward Martinez and left-winger Czibor. The Spaniards who were defending the trophy, made sure of keeping it with further goals from Czibor (48 minutes) and right-winger Coll (78 minutes) Harry Hooper scored Birmingham's goal eight minutes from time when goalkeeper Ramallets fisted the left-winger's shot into his own net. Birmingham often upset the fans with many fouls. Brian Farmer had his name taken and left-back George Allen brought roars from the terraces when he kicked the ball into touch after bringing down right-half Vorses.

- LOST 1–4 ON AGGREGATE

1960–61

Round 1 First Leg

- 19 October 1960 v Ujpesti Dozsa (Hungary), Home 3–2 Attendance 23,381
- SCHOFIELD, FARMER, ALLEN, WATTS, SISSONS, NEAL, HELLAWELL, RUDD, GORDON (2), SINGER, ASTALL(1).

UJPESTI DOZSA - BUDAPEST
Back Row—Kuharszky, Nagy, Gorocs, Varhidi, Gyorvari, Torok
Front Row—Rajna, Szini, Borsanyi, Szusza, Toth

Ujpesti Dozsa Team Group 1960

Round 1 Second Leg

- 26 October 1960 v Ujpesti Dozsa (Hungary), Away 2–1 Attendance 25,000
- SCHOFIELD, FARMER, ALLEN, WATTS, SMITH, NEAL, HELLAWELL, BARLOW, GORDON, SINGER (1), RUDD (1).
- WON 5–3 ON AGGREGATE

Round 2 First Leg

- 23 November 1960 v Boldklub Copenhagen (Denmark), Away 4–4 Attendance 2,500
- SCHOFIELD, FARMER, ALLEN, WATTS, SMITH, NEAL, HELLAWELL, GORDON (2), SINGER (2), BLOOMFIELD, TAYLOR.

Round 2 Second Leg

- 7 December 1960 v Boldklub Copenhagen (Denmark), Home 5–0 Attendance 22,486
- WITHERS, FARMER, ALLEN, WATTS, SISSONS, NEAL, HELLAWELL (1), STUBBS(2), HARRIS (1), BLOOMFIELD (1), TAYLOR.

Match Report from *Daily Mirror,* 8 December 1960:

HARRIS STARTS CUP SPREE

Birmingham City, determined to reach the semi-final of the Inter-Cities Cup for the third successive time, got off to a flying start against this Copenhagen side. With only five minutes of this quarter-final second-leg gone, they took the lead. And the man who set the Birmingham fans roaring was inside-right Robin Stubbs, 19.

Taking a short pass from outside-left Brian Taylor, Stubbs cut inside and let fly from fifteen yards. The ball flashed into the net off a defender. Birmingham were lucky when right-half Johnny Watts kicked a shot from outside-left Mortensen off the line. But then the Danes were shattered by a sensational three goals in five minutes burst.

New boy Harris started it with a brilliant forty-eighth minute goal. He raced past two other bewildered defenders to crash home an unstoppable shot. Two minutes later outside-right Mike Hellawell seized on to a loose ball and his shot flashed into the net. In the fifty-third minute Jimmy Bloomfield weaved his way through and his shot was deflected home by right-back Henning Helbrandt. Stubbs hammered home number five in the 67th minute.

- WON 9–4 ON AGGREGATE

Semi-Final First Leg
- 19 April 1961 v Internazionale (Italy), Away 2–1 Attendance: 18,000
- WITHERS, FARMER, ALLEN, HENNESSEY, SMITH, NEAL, HELLAWELL, STUBBS, HARRIS (1), BLOOMFIELD, ORRITT.
- BALLERI Own Goal

Match Report from *Daily Mirror* Thursday 20 April 1961 by Ken Jones:
Italians scorched by fans in sun-drenched Milan
BIRMINGHAM SET FOR 'FAIRS' FINAL
The piercing whistle of derision echoed round the giant San Corso Stadium here in Milan today as lire-rich Internazionale crashed 2–1 to Birmingham City in the sun-drenched first leg of the Inter-Cities Fairs Cup semi-final. Angered by a shattering run of five defeats that has toppled them off the top of the Italian League, the Internazionale fans saw their team crash again. And there was no fluke about a prestige boosting Birmingham win that amazingly must rank as one of their easiest of the season – and one which puts them in with a great chance of qualifying for the final in the second leg at Birmingham on 3 May.

Inspired by some brilliant inside-forward play from Jimmy Bloomfield and a give-nothing-away defence, Birmingham had the whip hand until they faded in the stamina-sapping heat towards the end. But by then they had a 2–0 lead that was good enough to win the game, even though Eddie Firmani, former Charlton Athletic forward, scored nine minutes from time. The man who had a hand in both of Birmingham's goals was Welsh wing-half starlet, 18-year-old Terry Hennessey. It was Hennessey who sparked off a 12th minute move that set Bloomfield off on a run to open the way for centre-forward Jimmy Harris to get the first. Four minutes from half-time, Hennessey slung a long ball down the right-wing for Mike Hellawell. Hellawell crossed to Harris whose header was going wide when Internazionale left-half Balleri headed into his own net.

Birmingham, banking on defence in the second half had some anxious moments and goalkeeper Colin Withers made a great point-blank save from Firmani in the closing minutes.

Semi-Final Second Leg
- 3 May 1961 v Internazionale (Italy), Home 2–1 Attendance: 29,530
- SCHOFIELD, FARMER, ALLEN, HENNESSEY, SMITH, NEAL, HELLAWELL, ORRITT, HARRIS (2), BLOOMFIELD, AULD.
- WON 4–2 ON AGGREGATE

Match Report from *Daily Mirror* 4 May 1961:
Auld helps Birmingham Through to Final of Fairs Cup
TWO-GOAL HARRIS BLASTS ITALIANS
Bertie Auld, signed from Glasgow Celtic for £15,000 only forty-eight hours before this match, made a dream debut for City last night. The dark-haired left-winger created two chances for goal-snatching centre-forward Jimmy Harris to take the Midlanders into the Final of the Inter-Cities Fairs Cup.

Auld's speed and shooting ability impressed the home fans, and he had them cheering with his first three opening minutes. His hard shot was punched out by 'keeper Buffon. Left-half Dick Neal crashed the clearance against the post and Harris scored from the rebound.

In the sixty-fifth minute Auld was brought down by Milan's right-back, Gatti, and from his hard, low cross Harris scored with a diving header. The Scots lad certainly looks like solving Birmingham's problem position, and he was unlucky not to score himself.

Twice he had power drives charged down and then he saw a brilliant header flash inches over. This is the second time in four years Birmingham have been in the final. Inside-left Jimmy Bloomfield gave a masterly show of ball control and there was far more bite from the other forwards as well. Buffon made some brilliant saves , but Birmingham's 'keeper, Johnny Schofield was shaky.

The clever Italian forwards, however, never really troubled the sound, well-packed home defence. Only twice did they look like scoring. Centre-half Trevor Smith kicked a shot from Eddie Firmani off the line. Then right back Brain Farmer cleared another attempt from right-winger Masiero with Schofield beaten. It was the little winger who eventually pulled the Italians back into the game with a cracking twenty-yard shot after 67 minutes. But the Italians couldn't pull out enough fire to stop Birmingham from meeting either Roma or Hibernian in the final, which will be played early next season.

Blues Team Group for Final in 1961

Final First Leg
- 27 September 27 1961 v AS Roma (Italy), Home 2–2 Attendance: 21,005
- SCHOFIELD, FARMER, SISSONS, HENNESSEY, FOSTER, BEARD, HELLAWELL (1), BLOOMFIELD, HARRIS, ORRITT (1), AULD.

Final Second Leg
- October 11 1961 v AS Roma (Italy), Away 0-2 Attendance: 50,000
- SCHOFIELD, FARMER, SISSONS, HENNESSEY, SMITH, BEARD, HELLAWELL, BLOOMFIELD, HARRIS, SINGER, ORRITT.

Programme 27th September 1961

Match Report from *Daily Mirror*, 12 October 1961 by Ken Jones:
Touchline Clash After Roma Manager Holds Up Big Game
MERRICK IN A CUP TUSSLE AS 'BRUM' CRASH
Luis Carniglia, fiery Roma boss, had to be hauled back to the trainer's bench in the giant Olympic Stadium here today after a sensational touchline tussle with Birmingham manager Gil Merrick.

Over 50,000 fans – including new F.I.F.A. president Sir Stanley Rous – saw this explosive Inter-Cities Fairs Cup Final blow up in the twenty-fifth minute when angry Carniglia raced on to the pitch for the second time in the game. Carniglia pushed and shoved Birmingham players and then clashed with Merrick who had followed him from the bench.

Angered by a Trevor Smith tackle on right-winger Orlando – one that didn't even rate a free-kick from French referee Schwinte – Carniglia refused to let the game continue as he charged around demanding justice. Merrick who was forced to defend himself, stood amazed while Carniglia was led away by other Roma officials.

After the game, which gave Roma the cup on a 4–2 home-and-away aggregate the Birmingham manager told me: "This man had already been on the field once. He looked as though he was going to strike one or two of my players and I went after him to try and avoid an incident. I am still amazed by it all."

The Italian manager had nearly sparked off an incident after only ten minutes. He ran sixty yards to push away Birmingham skipper Jimmy Bloomfield, who was bending over an injured Roma player.

But I refuse to fault Birmingham – so often labelled "Brum Bashers" – for a series of incidents that spoiled this final.

They amazingly kept their control as the Italians used every trick of body checking and obstruction to make things run their way. Sadly the biggest offender was South American inside-left Lojacano, the outstanding performer in the game. This swarthy star out-generalled the Birmingham team, who are struggling at the bottom of the First Division. But the fiery temper that has earned Lojacano the nickname of the "wild one" in Italy, continually spoiled a superb performance.

Birmingham's goalkeeper Johnny Schofield gave a brilliant display to keep Roma out until the 62nd minute. Then Lojacano, tired of the failings of his fellow forwards, started the move which ended with Birmingham full-back Brian Farmer putting the ball into his own net. Birmingham, outplayed for most of the game, still had their chances. In a five minute spell after Roma scored, both centre-forward Jimmy Harris and left-winger Brian Orritt scooped shots wide. Then Roma took complete charge again. Centre-forward Manfredini missed three golden chances. But Roma made sure of the Cup in injury time when left-half Pestrin crashed in a long shot that dipped into the top corner of the net.

- LOST 2–4 ON AGGREGATE

1961–62

Round 1 – Bye
Round 2 First Leg
- 15 November 15 1961 v RCD Espanol (Spain), Away 2–5 Attendance: 60,000
- SCHOFIELD, LYNN, SISSONS, HENNESSEY, SMITH, BEARD, HELLAWELL, BLOOMFIELD (1), HARRIS (1 Penalty), ORRITT, AULD.

Round 2 Second Leg
- 7 December 1961 v RCD Espanol (Spain), Home 1–0 Attendance: 16,874
- SCHOFIELD, LYNN, SISSONS, HENNESSEY, SMITH, BEARD, HELLAWELL, ORRITT, HARRIS, LEEK, AULD.

EUROPA LEAGUE
On 27 February 2011 against all odds Blues won the League Cup sponsored by Carling 2-1 against Arsenal at Wembley and therefore qualified for European competition for the first time in 50 years.

As is usual with Blues things are never quite as straightforward as they should be and a cloud hung over St Andrew's as to whether we would be able to participate in the UEFA Europa League due to the financial position of the club. The Sport section of the *Daily Telegraph* wrote:

"Uncertainty over the ability of Birmingham City's parent company to continue as a going concern prompted suggestions that the club's place in UEFA's Europa League next season, secured by beating Arsenal in the Carling Cup Final, could be in jeopardy.

UEFA delegates its licensing scheme to national associations, and under disclosure rules brought in after the collapse of Portsmouth last year, Birmingham needed to provide written assurance that they can meet their liabilities for the year ahead and that loans will not be called in to satisfy the FA and the Premier League.

The Premier League admitted that they have been closely monitoring Birmingham and the club's licence could have been refused by the Football Association, unless Birmingham's owner, Carson Yeung could prove their future is secure. But representatives from the governing bodies have now decreed that Birmingham ought to be allowed to play in Europe. Acting Chairman Peter Pannu said, "We can all look forward to competing in the Europa League alongside some of the continent's finest clubs. Being granted the licence – which were always confident of achieving – will put to rest once and for all some of the scare mongering that has surrounded the club"

After 50 years absence from European competition meant that for the majority of Bluenoses this was a first-time experience and one not to be missed by those in their 60s who recalled those halcyon days when European travel was not that easy with limited flights to the continent from Elmdon Airport.

Blues Results were:

PLAY OFFS

* 18 August 2011 NACIONAL 0–0 Birmingham, Stadium: Estadio da Madeira, Funchal Portugal Referee: Milorad Mazic (SRB)

Match Report *Birmingham Mail*, Friday 19 August 2011 by Colin Tattum in Madeira:

UNLUCKY BLUES KNOCK ON WOOD

Oh-So Close To A Dream Result On European Return

Birmingham City's grand European adventure got off to a good start that could have been great. Blues hit the woodwork three times against Portugese opponents Nacional and performed with superb control and drive. All that was missing was the goal – or two. Chris Wood (twice) and Steven Caldwell were the unfortunates who were denied by the woodwork. Nacional ran out of ideas pretty quickly as Blues dictated for long swathes of the Europa League tie. Blues, in fact, looked as comfortable as any seasoned European campaigners might.

It's been 50 years since Blues competed on this stage and on last night's evidence they can be confident of finishing the job off in the play-off second leg at St Andrew's next Thursday. You would have been hard-pressed to predict this as the Blues team to take to the European stage after they lifted the Carling Cup. Just two players from that Wembley starting XI lined up at the Estadio da Madeira – Stephen Carr, on his 100th appearance for Blues – and Liam Ridgewell.

In the months since qualification for Europe was secured by that famous victory over Arsenal, the club has been plunged into crisis on and off the field.

And Ridgewell's inclusion was in an unusual role: the anchor midfielder. Ridgewell sat in the middle of Jean Beausejour and Jonathan Spector, who was making his Blues debut. Nathan Redmond and Chris Burke occupied the flanks, with Wood the lone striker.

There was no Jordan Mutch or Morgaro Gomis due to injury, and there was no place on the substitutes bench for Scott Dann, who didn't train the evening before when Blues arrived on Madeira. Although it was an unusual, if not makeshift, Blues side it wasn't particularly shown in an opening period when they twice hit the woodwork. Ridgewell did a very good job as the pivot and Beausejour oozed class throughout.

Nacional, fielding their strongest side, started brightly and were it not for a superb tackle from behind from Curtis Davies in the eighth minute, Mateus would have put the hosts ahead. Blues settled down and in the 24th minute came close to taking the lead when a corner deep to the far post was met firmly by Caldwell. His header was carefully directed downwards but rebounded back off the base of Elisson's upright. Davies, again, was on hand to snuff out danger by producing a block tackle to stop Mario Rondon turning in a cross at the near post.

But for all their busy manner and technical ability, Nacional flattered to deceive and Blues gradually began to take control of the first half, and ultimately the game.

A minute before the break they came agonisingly close once more to breaking the deadlock, from a curving Beausejour free-kick from the left into the penalty area. Davies crashed into Elisson as he flapped at the ball and it popped back to Wood 15 yards out. He let rip with a stinging half-volley but the ball cannoned off the underside of the crossbar and was hastily cleared by Nacional's defence.

Nacional made two changes for the second half but before they could take any effect Blues had them on the back foot. Two minutes after the change round Redmond teased and then cut inside Joao Aurelio before curling a low shot that Elisson just about touched round.

After Blues recovered the ball from the subsequent corner, Burke floated a cross into the thick of things and Wood peeled off and planted a firm header past Elisson but on to the post.

Nacional seemed caught cold by the verve Blues were performing with. And as Blues' confidence grew, Nacional took on the look of a dispirited and frustrated outfit. Thrills and spills were few and far between after that near miss, with Blues ensuring they did nothing silly and make a slip from their position of dominance.

A lovely curling ball from David Murphy skidded beyond Felipe Lopes and allowed Wood the chance to run in from an angle. He fired a left-footer from a tight angle that zipped across the face of Elisson's goal. Blues never allowed Nacional to wrestle any control thereafter and at the end could have finally got the reward their performance deserved.

Another teasing Beausejour free-kick caused problems and Caldwell rose above everybody, but his header had a little too much elevation on it and it sailed over the crossbar.

The Teams:

- CD NACIONAL: Ellisson, Aurelio, Pinto, Danielson, Lopes, Mihelic (Diego, ht), Alberto, Skolnik (Elizeu, ht), Da Costa (Candeias, 69), Rondon, Mateus. Substitutes: Valverde, Todorovic, Barcelos, Minatel, Neto.
- BLUES: Myhill (7), Carr (7), Murphy (7), Caldwell (7), Davies (8), Ridgewell (7), Burke (7), BEAUSEJOUR * (8), Spector (7), Redmond (7), Wood (7) Substitutes: Doyle, Rooney, Valles, Asante, Jervis, Hubbins.

25 August 2011 BIRMINGHAM 3–0 NACIONAL, Stadium: St. Andrew's Referee: Vladislav Bezborodov (RUS) Crowd: 27,698

Match Report

Birmingham registered one of the great achievements in the club's history as they saw off Portugese side CD Nacional 3–0 to qualify for the group stages of the UEFA Europa League.

Following a goalless first leg in Madeira in which Blues hit the woodwork three times, the Midlands outfit struck twice in nine first-half minutes to take firm control of the tie.

Nathan Redmond, David Murphy and Chris Wood scored the goals as Chris Hughton's men claimed a relatively straightforward win.

The visitors' clearest opportunity to strike an early blow came as Curtis Davies misjudged a long goal-kick from Rosa Elisson. Mateus nicked in to nudge the ball past 'keeper Boaz Myhill on the edge of the box, only to be forced back to David Candelas – who curled wide.

It was certainly against the run of play when Blues opened the scoring in the 15th minute, but it was a goal of pure quality. Left-back Murphy fed Redmond and the youngster skipped past Luis Alberto before drilling into the bottom corner from 20 yards.

The goal certainly settled Blues and lifted the home support, who were in dreamland soon after. Jean Beausejour's inswinging corner was met at the near post by a combination of Murphy and Alberto and the ball found the net via the crossbar. Birmingham were in full swing and Wood was only denied a third by a last-ditch block from Zarko Tomasevic.

Nacional remained a threat in attack but it was Blues who went close to scoring every time they went forward, Chris Burke seeing his effort cleared off the line by Ferreira Claudemir before Adam Rooney's side-footed volley forced a solid save from Elisson.

Rooney enjoyed a clear chance to wrap matters up in the 77th minute, but Wood in acres of space, opted to shoot straight at Elisson.

Redmond then curled against the far post before Wood, who had minutes earlier seen his attempted chip saved by Elisson, rounded off a memorable night from close range following a swift counter.

The Teams

- BLUES: Myhill, Carr, Spector, Caldwell, Davies, Murphy, Burke (Asante 88), Beausejour, Redmond, Rooney, Wood (Jervis 88) Substitutes: Doyle, Hancox, Kerr, Fahey.
- NACIONAL: Elisson, Claudemir (Costa 55), Danielson, Tomasevic, Felipe, Alberto, Eliseu, Diego (Mihelic 55) , Rondon, Mateus (Minatel 64), Candeias Substitutes: Valverde, Skolnik, Todorovic, Pinto.

Bookings:

- BLUES: Carr (74).
- NACIONAL: Mateus (32) Candeias (54)
- BLUES WON 3–0 ON AGGREGATE

GROUP STAGE (GROUP H)

- 15 September 2011
- Birmingham 1 Braga 3, Stadium: St Andrew's, Referee: Deniz Aytekin (GER)

Match Report *Birmingham Mail* Friday 16 September 2011 by Colin Tattum:

NO SHAME IN VALIENT DEFEAT

Braga Pushed All The Way By Battling Blues

Blues came off St Andrew's with honour and pride in defeat. SC Braga's quality told at key moments and although Blues pushed them all the way, rousing for a big hurrah at the end to put the opening Group H game back in the balance, it was just an ask too much.

Marlon King registered his first goal for the club, capping a Man of the Match performance, in the 71st minute. And that lifted Blues to go again and mount such a strong finish, with Nathan Redmond only denied what would have been a spectacular equaliser by Quim's flying save.

As it was, Braga iced their first European victory on English soil with a breakaway goal with two minutes to go that was tough on Blues. With an eye on Sunday's match at in-form Southampton, Chris Hughton made some swingeing changes. There were seven in all, and four players making starting debuts; Pablo, Wade Elliott, Guirane N'Daw and King. And it showed in a first half that was shaped by an early incident at either end within a space of 60 seconds.

King skipped away from a challenge on the right and scampered towards the Braga area as an expectant St Andrew's roared him on. He crossed low and Adam Rooney seemed to get just too far ahead of the ball and side-footed it wide of the near post. Rooney connected with the "wrong" foot, his left, when a touch with the other would surely have swept it in. As Blues' fans agonised, Braga promptly worked the ball into a good position on the left and took the lead. Elderson curled the ball into the Blues penalty area and Helder Barbosa caught it sweetly on the volley from 16 yards. The ball arched at speed and although Boaz Myhill got fingertips on it, his was not a strong enough touch to stop the ball's path into the net, off the underside of the crossbar.

It was a deflating blow for Blues, and the first goal they have conceded at St Andrew's this season.

Braga then proceeded to dictate as Blues, with Pablo and N'Daw looking lost and suspect on occasions and trying to find their rhythm, wobbled, but held in there. Myhill pushed away a Hugo Viana free-kick and Blues had to withstand a lot of pressure as the Portugese, sharp and slippery in possession in the final third, tried to make matters worse.

Redmond tested Quim with a curler from the right and Rooney glanced an Elliott free-kick just over as Blues gradually began to find themselves, and get a measure of the opposition. King's presence and intelligence was encouraging, not least for the months to come, and he kept Braga's defence on their toes with a bristling, vibrant display. Blues needed to build on their good parts from the opening half, but they never quite got properly into gear immediately after the change-around.

And when Braga scored a second goal in the 59th minute, the game looked to have been killed as a contest. Elderson crossed the ball to the far post where David Murphy and Nuno Gomes flew in. It spun back off them as they slid in together invitingly for Lima, who was offside when Elderson delivered the original pass. Left free, he cracked a left-footer into the top corner with Myhill not getting the merest sniff due to its sheer power.

Chris Wood and Chris Burke were immediately sent on, N'Daw's difficult debut brought to an end. Elliott was moved into central midfield alongside Jonathan Spector and Burke went to the right – and his impact was sudden.

With 19 minutes left, Burke burrowed away and manoeuvred himself on the outside of his full-back; going into the right-hand side of the penalty area. He unleashed a cross-shot and with the Braga defence stood till, King ran round the 'keeper to tap the ball into the unguarded goal. Suddenly Blues had a lifeline and with King showing relentless energy and willing and Burke adding extra danger, the team and crowd roused.

An Elliott cross from the right was collected by Redmond and he fired in a shot that was headed just wide of his own goal by Paulo Vinicius. And then in the 81st minute Redmond produced a moment of magic to almost bring Blues level as they piled the pressure on. Taking a ball that had been well switched from an attack on the opposite flank, he steadied himself and struck a brilliant first-time curler from 30 yards that seemed to be destined for the top corner, but Quim acrobatically clawed it out and away – an audacious attempt and a fine save.

With four mminutes to go the excellent Murphy gently lifted a free-kick just over the crossbar as Blues finished with a flourish, but came valiantly short. With two minutes left Braga got a third.

Carlao was played through, onside according to the linesman, and took his time before squaring to Helder Barbosa to hammer the ball past Myhill from close range.

The Teams
- BLUES: Myhill (7), Carr (5), Murphy (7), Pablo (6), Ridgewell (7), Elliott (6), N'Daw (5) (Burke 60 (7)), Spector (7), Redmond (7), KING (7*), Rooney (6) (Wood 60 (6)). Substitutes: Doyle, Caldwell, Beausejour, Davies, Asante.
- BRAGA: Quim, Baiano, Ewerton, Paulo Vinicius, Elderson, Djamal, Hugo Viana, Helder Barbosa, Lima (Carlao, 83), Alan, Nuno Gomes (Salino, 73). Substitutes: Berni, Imorou, Mossoro, Merida, Paulo Cesar.

29 September 2011 Maribor 1 Blues 2 Stadium: Stadion Liudski vrt Maribor (SVN), Referee: Tom Harald Hagen (NOR)

Match Report *Birmingham Mail* Friday 30 September 2011 by Colin Tattum in Maribor:

DOYLE HEAVES A SIGH OF RELIEF

Blues Transform Euro Tie After A 'Keeper Calamity

An historic evening for Blues that was all set to be nothing but a horrific one.

Not least for Colin Doyle, who did an Enckelman as Blues Europa League dreams appeared completely shattered. Doyle's airshot at a poor, short back pass by Johnathan Spector handed the Slovenian league leaders the initiative.

But as Blues laboured as the Group H match wore on, they suddenly struck through Chris Burke in the 64th minute and forced their will on their hosts to devastating effect.

Wade Elliott plundered the winner with an opportunist 25-yarder with 11 minutes to go and Blues recovery from being so down at heel was quite remarkable.

Blues made five changes to their side, with Doyle coming into goal for his first taste of European action and Liam Ridgewell taking the captain's armband. Elliott was given a new role, playing just behind Marlon King, and it eventually paid dividends. Their initial start to the match was solid and steady but Maribor began to move Blues about and got their eye in on Doyle's goal. First Marcos Tavares fired wide from a good position after bumping Steven Caldwell away from a long diagonal ball. And Doyle palmed away a free header from Goran Cvijanovic at full stretch before Blues regained a foothold.

King could have been played clean through but Elliott's return pass was much too heavy, and minutes before Doyle's embarrassment Fahey squandered an opportunity to open the scoring. Jasmin Handanovic did well to get a punch on a cross that King was about to nod in and Fahey lashed the follow-up high and wide from outside the box after it bounced back his way.

Then the Enckelman moment turned the game upside down, and left Blues in a state of shock. Spector did Doyle no favours with a very casual back pass that he dinked, with very little pace on it. The ball bobbled towards Doyle and instead of going through it with his left foot, he tried to readjust and clear with

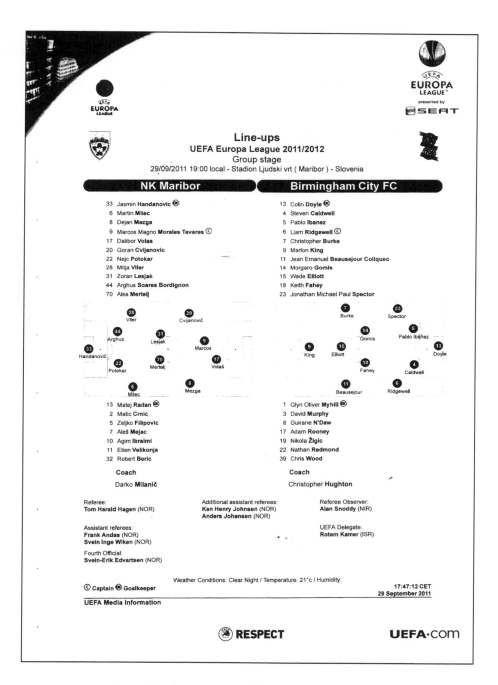

Line-ups
UEFA Europa League 2011/2012
Group stage
29/09/2011 19:00 local - Stadion Ljudski vrt (Maribor) - Slovenia

NK Maribor	Birmingham City FC
33 Jasmin **Handanovic** (GK)	13 Colin **Doyle** (GK)
6 Martin **Milec**	4 Steven **Caldwell**
8 Dejan **Mezga**	5 Pablo **Ibanez**
9 Marcos Magno **Morales Tavares** (C)	6 Liam **Ridgewell** (C)
17 Dalibor **Volas**	7 Christopher **Burke**
20 Goran **Cvijanovic**	9 Marlon **King**
22 Nejc **Potokar**	11 Jean Emanuel **Beausejour Coliqueo**
28 Mitja **Viler**	14 Morgaro **Gomis**
31 Zoran **Lesjak**	15 Wade **Elliott**
44 Arghus **Soares Bordignon**	18 Keith **Fahey**
70 Ales **Mertelj**	23 Jonathan Michael Paul **Spector**

13 Matej **Radan** (GK)	1 Glyn Oliver **Myhill** (GK)
2 Matic **Crnic**	3 David **Murphy**
5 Zeljko **Filipovic**	8 Guirane **N'Daw**
7 Aleš **Mejac**	17 Adam **Rooney**
10 Agim **Ibraimi**	19 Nikola **Žigic**
11 Etien **Velikonja**	22 Nathan **Redmond**
32 Robert **Beric**	39 Chris **Wood**

Coach	**Coach**
Darko **Milanič**	Christopher **Hughton**

Referee:
Tom Harald Hagen (NOR)

Additional assistant referees:
Ken Henry Johnsen (NOR)
Anders Johansen (NOR)

Referee Observer:
Alan Snoddy (NIR)

Assistant referees:
Frank Andas (NOR)
Svein Inge Wiken (NOR)

UEFA Delegate:
Rotem Kamer (ISR)

Fourth Official:
Svein-Erik Edvartsen (NOR)

Weather Conditions: Clear Night / Temperature: 21°c / Humidity:

17:47:12 CET
29 September 2011

(C) Captain (GK) Goalkeeper

UEFA Media Information

RESPECT   UEFA·com

UEFA Media Kit Line Up for 29th September 2011

his right as it went across him and only succeeded in getting in a muddle. He lashed at fresh air, the ball bounced on and as Dalibor Volas gleefully nipped onto it to score, Doyle stopped, rooted to the spot in horror. What a calamity, and it will be a moment that Doyle will find hard to live down, coming on such a big stage and a big night for Blues as well.

Blues struggled to react and get it out of their system in the remainder of the first-half and it was five minutes before the interval that they troubled Handanovic, through a stinging Burke shot that he parried away firmly. It looked as if Blues were meandering nowhere but in the 64th minute a sudden break caused panic for Maribor – and an equaliser for Blues.

The ball rebounded forward from Blues territory as they cleared in midfield and rolled to King, who showed strength to keep it and then reverse it into Burke's path. Maribor's defence were all at sea and Burke nicked the ball round Martin Melic's desperate diving lunge and ran around to collect, and advance on Handanovic.

Burke coolly slotted a sidefooter into the bottom corner, with just enough sting on it as the 'keeper came out and got a hand on the shot. The 800 or so travelling fans went wild with delirium and the goal came just as Hughton had got Nikola Zigic and Chris Wood stripped and waiting to come on. The goal meant that Wood was told to sit back down but Zigic entered the fray and immediately made his presence felt, heading over a glorious chance from close range.

Buoyed and on their uppers, Blues now appeared the team most likely to score again. In the 73rd minute Elliott wriggled into a position where he could see the whites of Handanovic's eyes. But he couldn't quite get a shot away as he wanted under pressure from a defender, and the 'keeper made a vital save from a prodded attempt. But Elliott fared better, with a little help from Handanovic, to dramatically fire Blues into the lead with 11 minutes left. A hooked clearance downfield by Caldwell dropped to Morgaro Gomis as Maribor's defence tried to come up and out. He had one defender to beat and appealed for handball as he tried to flip it past his opponent but before any judgement could be made, Elliott made it immaterial. Latching onto the loose ball, he let rip first-time from outside the Maribor penalty area and his shot squirmed through the grasp of Handanovic as he tried to smother it.

A remarkable change in fortune; Blues transformed themselves and watchfully and carefully saw out the remaining time to secure an historic Europa League victory.

The Teams

- NK MARIBOR: (4-1-4-1) Handanovic, Milec, Viller, Arghus, Potokar, Mezga (Crnic 86), Mertelj (Beric 81), Lesjak, Volas, Tavares, Cvijanovic (Ibraimi, 71). Substitutes: Radan, Filipovic, Mejac, Vellikonja.
- BLUES: (4-4-1-1) Doyle (5), Spector (5), Ridgewell (5), Caldwell (6), Pablo (6), Burke (6), Gomis (5), Fahey (5), Elliott (6), King (6) (Zigic 65 (6)), BEAUSEJOUR (6*). Substitutes: Myhill, Murphy, N'Daw, Rooney, Redmond, Wood.
- Booked: Ridgewell (44, shirt pull) and Gomis (60, foul)

20 October 2011 Club Brugge 1 Blues 2 Stadium: Jan Brevdelstadion Bruges (BEL), Referee: Daniele Orsato (ITA).

Match Report *Birmingham Mail* Friday 21 October 21 2011 by Colin Tattum in Bruges:
A NIGHT TO SAY 'I WAS THERE'
Blue Army Hails A Last-Minute Wood Winner
In Bruges and in dreamland. Blues European adventure took another incredible twist on a night of drama unparalleled in club history.

Chris Wood scored the winner in the 10th minute of stoppage-time to secure a come-from-behind victory. But more than that and the joint lead of Group H in the Europa League were the circumstances. Blues appeared shaken by a terrible facial injury to Pablo, which accounted for the extra minutes.

But they summoned one last hurrah deep into added time to leave Club Brugge reeling.

And with it they made light of a slow start that cost them the initiative. But once David Murphy had equalised Joseph Akpala's goal, Chris Hughton's men thoroughly deserved their reward from the late drama, as did the travelling army of 5,500 supporters who provided an electric backdrop that had the Jan Breydel Stadion rocking. It all appeared so different at first.

Blues' start was frustratingly poor, and they paid the price. They looked half-asleep and like a team that had six changes and were getting used to one another and their surroundings. They were too stand-offish and allowed Club Brugge easy possession. The hosts scored via an attack down the right through Nabil Dirar, who crossed low towards the six-yard box. Pablo slipped and Akpala got across him to deftly turn the ball on and past Boaz Myhill. Blues just didn't look at it or with it, yet when Murphy got the leveller, the transformation in the game was sharp and quite remarkable. It was a neat, clever goal too as there looked not a lot on as Blues came down the Club Brugge's left. Nikola Zigic had been flattened in the build up and only Adam Rooney was there in the penalty area to aim for but Jonathan Spector brushed aside his opponent to buy a little more time and support, and his low centre was met by Murphy at the far post. Murphy nipped inside the defender stationed furthest on the right like a veteran goal-poacher and steered the ball into the bottom corner from close range with a cool left-foot shot.

The south end of the stadium went wild and, with such incessant and cacophonous support behind them every step of the way, Blues grew in stature and Club Brugge looked a rattle lot. Zigic had a shot on the turn blocked and as the half wore on the yellow shirts of the away side kept coming again and again in swarms. On a counter-attack, Rooney played in Keith Fahey who should have let rip instead of trying to tee up Burke. Then, from a long throw down the line by Murphy that caught Tom Hogli out, Rooney went clear only to lash a sliced shot across the far post and wide. Blues had their tails up and they continued to take the game to Club Brugge. Three minutes before the interval a Murphy centre was cushioned down to Rooney by Zigic and although his attempt from 10 yards was snaffled by the goalkeeper, he appeared to be bundled over from behind, but no penalty was given. Club Brugge began the second period more composed and with renewed vigour. But Blues were equal to them and in the 59th minute should have taken the lead when Spector and Burke fashioned an opening from the right that lopped over to Zigic. Unmarked, he had time to plant his header where he so wished – but agonisingly it flashed wide of the post. What a chance, what a miss.

Club Brugge brought on Jimmy De Jonghe at left-back to try and stop the threat from that right-hand avenue and also Thomas Meunier to give Blues something else to think about on that flank going the other way. Wood and Marlon King replaced Blues' front two for the final 17 minutes and the game took on a nip and tuck feel.

The finale to the match threatened to be muted and not grandstand after Pablo suffered a horrific facial injury after he was felled by Akpala as they jumped for a cross. Pablo was already unconscious when he hit the ground with a thump after Akpala headed his cheek and there were frantic calls for medics to attend the stricken Spaniard.

Guirane n'Daw was in tears and Burke looked absolutely distraught at what he had seen and after six minutes treatment on the pitch, Pablo was carried off on a spinal board. In the eighth minute of added time Blues almost scored when King switched the ball to an over-lapping Wade Elliott on the left and his whistled just wide.

Then, in one of the most amazing climaxes you could imagine, Blues surged forward again and this time applied the coup de gras, Wood lunging in to put King's cross past Colin Coosemans into the roof of the net. Cue an amazing explosion of joy from supporters in the south end, and Blues keep right on to new heights in Europe.

The Teams
- BRUGGE: (4-3-3) Coosemans, Hogli, Vansteenkiste (De jonghe 60), Donk, Almeback, Odjidja, Zimling, Blondel (Deschilder 82) Dirar, Akpala, Refaelov (Meunier 64). Substitutes: Dhoest, Vleminckx, Lestienne, Van Acker.
- BLUES: (4-4-2) Myhill (7), Spector (7), MURPHY (8*), Caldwell (7), Pablo (7), Burke (7), N'Daw (7) (Ridgewell 90), Fahey (7), Zigic (7) (Wood 73), Rooney (7) (King 73), Elliott (7). Substitutes: Doyle, Beausejour, Gomis, Redmond.
- Bookings: BRUGGE: Blondel (31 foul), Zimling (handball 67). BLUES: Zigic (35, foul), Spector (76, foul), Elliott (82, foul)

3 November 2011 Birmingham 2 Club Brugge 2 Stadium: St Andrew's, Referee: Marcin Borski (POL)

Match Report *Birmingham Mail* Friday November 4 2011 by Colin Tattum:
BLUES REFUSE TO LIE DOWN
King Keeps His Nerve To Save Precious Point
If nothing else, Europe and Blues never cease to amaze. Looking completely down and out, they staged a rousing comeback to keep the Europa League dream very much alive.

Second-half goals by Jean Beausejour and Marlon King, from the penalty spot, earned them a share of this key Group H showdown.

The way they lifted themselves and transformed the game from such a precarious position has to be commended, and they had Clubbe Brugge sweating in an exciting end-to-end second period.

Had Blues not been so ineffective to begin with and fed off an expectant crowd, it perhaps would have been a much more memorable European night. But that said, there is something about Blues in this competition. They only do drama – and it was here aplenty again after Club Brugge seemed in command with quickfire goals before the break. Blues again started sloppily, as they did in Belgium, with passes not finding their mark and more than a hint of nervousness.

It was that getting-to-know you period partly due to eight changes, but on this occasion Blues failed to settle and never really functioned going forward. Club Brugge had problems in defence without three of their regular back four because of injury and goalkeeper Vladan Kujovic making his debut for the dropped Colin Coosemans.

But they had an easy ride as Club Brugge came through a spell of Blues possession in the middle of the opening period to strike right at the end of the half.

The opening goal came from a right-wing corner that sailed over all the heads and into Thomas Meunier (39 minutes).

His control on the sidefoot and chest to tee himself up was superb, and he then lashed a volley gleefully in past Wade Ellliott who was covering the far post. It was a slack goal for Blues to concede. They had got caught out with the three Club Brugge bodies converging on the delivered corner just yards in front of Menunier. Worse was to some a minute before half-time as Blues ran out of options as they tried to keep the ball and seek an opening. Beausejour gave possession away in midfield and Club Brugge broke to devastating effect. The ball was slipped to Vais Odjidja down the right channel into the penalty area and he switched it back, square for Joseph Akpala to administer the final touch, a simple tap in. Blues never really hurt Club Brugge in the first-half and their best opportunity came from a free-kick by David Murphy. He connected sweetly with a left-foot curler and was unfortunate to see it slam back off the angle of the post and crossbar in the 26th minute. Nikola Zigic then nodded down and wide from a good position at the back post, but Blues just didn't have enough penetration or guile. The two-goal burst left Blues up against it and something drastic was needed. Ten minutes after the change round it came, courtesy of Beausejour, sweeping a chance that fell to him into the roof of the net. The goal came from a swinging cross from the right by Elliott that was taken on the chest of Zigic, who tried to swivel a shot on goal. Ryan Donk got a desperate block in but the ball popped out nicely to Beausejour and he stuck it away in emphatic fashion. It ignited Blues, re-energised the crowd, and all of a sudden Club Brugge were in a proper, blood and thunder tie.

Yet just 60 seconds later it could have been all over when Odjidja, from 25 yards, sidefooted a low shot that eluded a full-stretch Colin Doyle and bounced off the base of the post. Chris Hughton then made a triple substitution bringing on Marlon King, Chris Wood and Chris Burke designed to keep Blues in the ascendancy and turn the screw a little further. And with the game on an absolute knife-edge and St Andrew's baying, Guirane N'Daw came so close to equalising with a spectacular 35-yarder. After the ball was cleared to him he promptly punted it back, and it was a fine save by Kujovic that tipped the dipping volley onto the post. With 16 minutes left of what had turned into an absolutely pulsating encounter, Blues drew level, from the penalty spot. Donk up-ended Beausejoour on the left-hand edge of the box as the winger tried to go back on himself and turn the ex-Albion man. King duly did the honours by firing the penalty into the bottom left-hand corner. Blues pressed and pushed some more in search of a winner, but Club Brugge showed grit to ensure that they didn't once more surrender a winning position, which has been their habit of late.

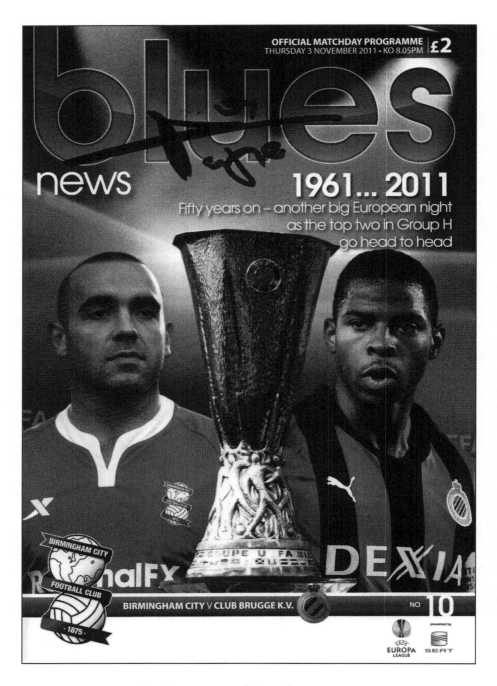

Programme 3rd November 2011

The Teams
- BLUES: (4-4-2) Doyle (6), Spector (6), MURPHY (7*), Caldwell (7), Pablo (7), Elliott (6) (Burke 66), Fahey (6), N'Daw (6), Zigic (5) (King 66), Rooney (5) (Wood 66), Beausejour (7). Substitutes: Myhill, Ridgewell, Redmond, Davies.
- CLUB BRUGGE: (4-3-3) Kujovic, Van Acker (Almeback 85), Vansteenkiste, Van Gijseghem, Donk, Zimling, Odjidja, Vazquez (Refaelov 81), Dirar, Akpala (Vleminckx 76), Meunier .Substitutes: Coosemans, Perdichizzi, Deschilder, De Jonghe

Bookings:
- BLUES: N'Daw (73, dissent)
- CLUB BRUGGE: Akpala (23, foul), Kujovic (63, time-wasting), Donk (64, foul), Vleminckx (90 + 3, handball)

30th November 2011 Braga 1 Blues 0 Stadium: Estadio Municipal de Braga (POR) Referee: Markus Strombergsson (SWE)

Match Report – Brian Cartlidge
Blues paid the price for Nikola Zigic's early saved penalty as a narrow 1–0 defeat in Braga means they now face an uphill battle in their bid to progress into the knock-out stages of the Europa League. The Serbian saw his 11th minute spot-kick saved by goalkeeper Quim and the Portugese hosts went on to claim victory thanks to a touch of fortune as Hugo Viana's 51st minute strike took a huge deflection off Curtis Davies.

The result sees Braga qualify for the final 32 from a tight Group H and means Blues must now defeat NK Maribor in the final round of fixtures and hope Club Brugge and Braga do not play out a draw which would see the Belgian side through.

Wade Elliott and Chris Burke enjoyed success in the early stages down the right channel and it was from that area that the former won a penalty for Blues when he was brought down by Ewerton on the edge of the box. However, Zigic saw the golden opportunity slip from his grasp as Quim dived to his left to produce a parried save.

Programme 30th November 2011

Braga steadied the ship after the early pressure and kept possession well, although only Marcio Mossoro went relatively close with a curled effort. Helder Barbosa passed up a great chance to test Boaz Myhill as half-time approached but he completely fluffed his attempted shot from Alan's low pass.

Keith Fahey could have made the Portuguese side pay at the other end but saw his low drive well swallowed up by Quim on the stroke of half-time.

Yet just minutes after half-time Chris Hughton's side saw all their good work unravelled thanks to a chunk of misfortune. Viana, formerly of Newcastle, received the ball 30 yards out and his left-footed effort took a huge deflection off the unfortunate Davies and wrong-footed Myhill. Barbosa was again guilty of missing a great opportunity when he fluffed his lines for a second time, on this occasion when trying to convert Mossoro's pass.

Marlon King and Burke got in each other's way when either man could have scored the equaliser while 10 minutes from time Rodrigo Lima was clean through on goal but denied by Myhill with Paulo Cesar somehow spooning the rebound over the bar.

The Teams

- BRAGA: Quim, Echiejile (Douglao 68), Ewerton, Mahamat, Vinicius, Viana, Barbosa (Cesar 68), Salino, Mossoro (Merida 84), Alan, Lima. Substitutes: Berni, Galo, Nuninho, Gomes.
- BLUES: Myhill, Spector, Davies, Caldwell, Murphy, N'Daw, Burke, Fahey, Beausejour (Redmond 64), Elliott (King 64), Zigic (Wood 76). Substitutes: Doyle, Pablo, Gomis, Rooney.

Bookings:

- BRAGA: Ewerton (1) Alan (87)
- BLUES: Caldwell (39) Burke (90)

15 December 2011 Blues 1 Maribor 0 Stadium: St Andrew's Referee: Sascha Kever (SUI) Crowd: 21,436

Match Report

Birmingham City did all that they could do to keep their European dream alive, but unfortunately a win was not enough to see them through to the knock out stage, as SC Braga failed to beat Club Bragge in the other Europa League Group H fixture.

Over 20,000 fans braved the cold to see Blues beat Maribor with a first-half strike from Adam Rooney – but it was out of their hands as to who progressed through the group. Chris Hughton made several changes to the side that beat Doncaster at the weekend. Rooney partnered Nikola Zigic up front, Doyle came in as 'keeper and Nathan Redmond was given the opportunity to start – to name but a few. In what is emerging as a familiar pattern, Blues dominated the first part of the game, seeming full of energy and enthusiasm for the challenge ahead.

Redmond immediately showed what he is capable of by firing a quality cross into the box but failed to find Zigic. NK Maribor had a brief chance, but it was very much Birmingham who were in control of the game and their superior play was rewarded within the first half-hour when Redmond's cross was met by Rooney who fired Birmingham in front. Despite taking the lead, Birmingham refused to sit back and continued to pressure Maribor with Zigic sending a shot wide just before half-time.

Blues came out positive again in the second half but the Birmingham fans were rocked by the news that Club Brugge had taken the lead against SC Braga. An eerie atmosphere surrounded the stadium as Blues fans now knew that no matter what the team did, progression to the next round was unlikely.

Birmingham were not deterred however and continued to boss the game. Nathan Redmond showing that he definitely one for the future with several teasing runs down the flank, not to mention some superb crosses as well as several shots on target himself.

NK Maribor were struggling to get possession and didn't appear threatening at all. Then news started to filter through that SC Braga had equalised and suddenly there was hope amongst the Blues fans again. Jordan Mutch came on to replace Rooney following a long absence due to a broken ankle and his return revved up the energy amongst the Blues fans – however the surreal atmosphere continued as Blues fans watched the game play out in front of them all the while focusing more on what was happening in the other game.

NK Maribor came as close as they had previously, but a strong challenge from Curtis Davies stopped the goal-scoring opportunity. With five minutes to go Redmond saw a fantastic shot hit the post before being taken off due to cramp, receiving a standing ovation as he left the pitch. Four minutes of injury time were displayed, but by this time Blues fans had heard the news that SC Braga had only managed a draw with Brugge – this ending Birmingham's European adventure.

Nevertheless, Blues fans rose to their feet at the end of the game and gave a rousing rendition of their anthem *"Keep Right On"* and applauded the team and the manager, thanking them for the wonderful adventure that they have taken them on.

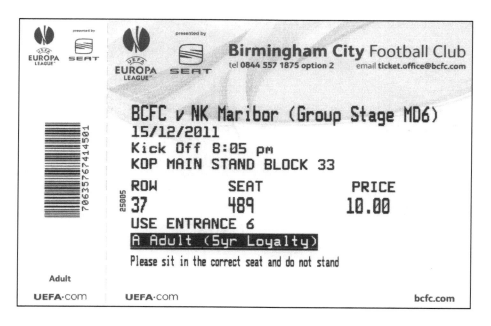

Ticket for match 15th December 2011

The Teams

- BLUES: Doyle, Pablo, Spector, Davies, Murphy, Fahey, Beausejour, Gomis (N'Daw 73), Redmond (Burke 88), Rooney (Mutch 88), Zigic. Substitutes: Myhill, Caldwell, Elliott, Wood.
- MARIBOR: Handanovic, Rajcevic, Potokar, Arghus (Trajkovski 75), Vidovic, Mezqa, Cvijanovic (Ibraimi 67), Merteli, Volas, Filipovic, Tavares (Velikonja 71). Substitutes: Radan, Milec, Lesjak, Beric.

Bookings:

- BLUES : Gomis (11) Murphy (70)
- MARIBOR: Vidovic (51) Arghus (59)

The Europa League Appearances (starts and substitutes) were:
(The figure in brackets is goals scored)
Boaz Myhill 3 (0)
Colin Doyle 3 (0)
Stephen Carr 1 (0)
David Murphy 5 (1)
Steven Caldwell 4 (0)
Pablo Ibanez 5 (0)
Liam Ridgewell 3 (0)
Curtis Davies 2 (0)
Chris Burke 6 (1)
Guirane N'Daw 5 (0)
Jean Beausejour 4 (1)
Jordan Mutch 1 (0)
Morgaro Gomis 2 (0)
Wade Elliott 5 (1)
Marlon King 5 (2)
Adam Rooney 4 (1)
Nikola Zigic 5 (0)
Chris Wood 4 (1)
Jonathan Spector 6 (0)
Nathan Redmond 3 (0)

GROUP H FINAL PLACINGS

				H			A			T					
		P	W	D	L	W	D	L	W	D	L	F	A	+/-	Pts
1	Brugge	6	1	1	1	2	1	0	3	2	1	12	9	3	11
2	Braga	6	2	0	1	1	2	0	3	2	1	12	6	6	11
3	Blues	6	1	1	1	2	0	1	3	1	2	8	8	0	10
4	Maribor	6	0	1	2	0	0	3	0	1	5	6	15	-9	1

EPILOGUE

So there we are, more than 50,000 words to justify that Birmingham City is a "better" club to support than Aston Villa.

There are some amongst you who did not need convincing and probably four times more that will never subscribe to the notion but hopefully there are one or two fathers who will use this book to justify their decision to take their children the Blue and White way with words like, "There you are I told you it was not as bad as all that."

KEEP RIGHT ON!